# VOCABULARY
# NINJA

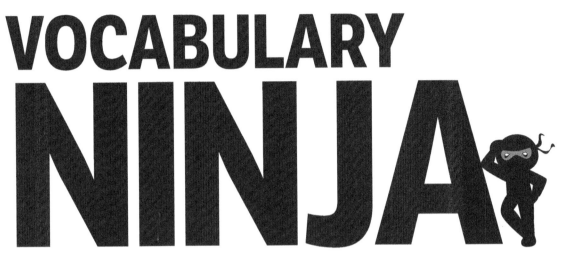

## A PHOTOCOPIABLE GUIDE TO TEACHING VOCABULARY IN PRIMARY

# ANDREW JENNINGS

## SECOND EDITION

BLOOMSBURY EDUCATION

LONDON OXFORD NEW YORK NEW DELHI SYDNEY

BLOOMSBURY EDUCATION
Bloomsbury Publishing Plc
50 Bedford Square, London, WC1B 3DP, UK
29 Earlsfort Terrace, Dublin 2, Ireland

BLOOMSBURY, BLOOMSBURY EDUCATION and the Diana logo are trademarks of
Bloomsbury Publishing Plc

First published in Great Britain, 2019 by Bloomsbury Publishing Plc

This edition published in Great Britain, 2024 by Bloomsbury Publishing Plc

Text copyright © Andrew Jennings, 2024

Andrew Jennings has asserted his right under the Copyright, Designs and Patents Act, 1988,
to be identified as Author of this work

A catalogue record for this book is available from the British Library

ISBN: PB: 978-1-8019-9437-8; ePDF: 978-1-8019-9439-2

2 4 6 8 10 9 7 5 3 1

Text design by Marcus Duck Design

Printed and bound in the UK by Ashford Education

To find out more about our authors and books visit www.bloomsbury.com and sign up
for our newsletters

## Acknowledgements

With thanks to Doug Harper for his kind permission to adapt extracts from
The Online Etymology Dictionary (www.etymonline.com) for the
Enthralling etymology section, page 59.

To my amazing wife, Claire, our special twins who changed everything for the better, and Max, Marmalade and Peaches. If only words could help me describe my love for you all.

# OTHER NINJA RESOURCES FOR TEACHERS

## COMPREHENSION NINJA NON-FICTION

A set of six books for ages 5–11 that provide carefully curated resources to teach the key reading comprehension skills. With strong links to the National Curriculum, each book presents 24 high-quality non-fiction texts and photocopiable activities that help embed reading skills and improve comprehension using strategies and question types such as true or false, labelling, matching, highlighting, filling in the gap, sequencing and multiple choice.

## COMPREHENSION NINJA FICTION AND POETRY

Each book in this six-book set contains 24 immersive fiction extracts and poetry texts by acclaimed writers including Roald Dahl, Michael Morpurgo, Patrice Lawrence, Katherine Rundell, David Almond, Zanib Mian, Joseph Coelho and Polly Ho-Yen. Every text is accompanied by photocopiable comprehension activities to boost reading retrieval skills in Key Stages 1 and 2.

# NINJA MATHS RESOURCES

## TIMES TABLES NINJA

### SARAH FARRELL WITH ANDREW JENNINGS

The activities in these photocopiable books give Key Stage 1 and Key Stage 2 pupils all the tools they need to gain fluency in multiplication and division. The KS1 book focuses on the 2, 3, 4, 5 and 10 times tables, while the KS2 book covers the 2 to 12 times tables in detail, ready for the Year 4 multiplication tables check.

## ARITHMETIC NINJA

### ANDREW JENNINGS WITH SARAH FARRELL AND PAUL TUCKER

The Arithmetic Ninja series is the perfect resource for any primary classroom. Ideal for daily maths practice and quick lesson starters, each photocopiable book includes 10 questions per day and 39 bonus weekly ninja challenges – 702 question cards in total.

# FOR CHILDREN AT HOME AND IN THE CLASSROOM

## WRITE LIKE A NINJA

A pocket-sized book packed full of all the grammar, vocabulary and sentence structures that children need in order to improve and develop their writing skills. Fully aligned to the Key Stage 2 National Curriculum, this book is designed to be used independently by pupils.

## SPELL LIKE A NINJA

This book provides essential tips, lists and advice to support the teaching and learning of spelling in the classroom or at home. Including every statutory spelling pattern in the National Curriculum, this all-in-one quick reference tool enables pupils to learn at their own pace.

# FURTHER RESOURCES FOR SCHOOLS, TEACHERS AND CHILDREN ONLINE

Head to www.vocabularyninja.co.uk and follow @VocabularyNinja on X (formerly Twitter) for more teaching and learning resources to support the teaching of vocabulary, reading, writing and the wider primary curriculum.

# CONTENTS

## PART ONE – THE WAY OF THE VOCABULARY NINJA

## PART TWO – VOCABULARY NINJA TOOLKIT

## PART THREE – BE THE VOCABULARY NINJA

# PART 1
## THE WAY OF THE VOCABULARY NINJA

# 1 – WELCOME, GRASSHOPPER

Welcome, Grasshopper

## WHY SHOULD YOU READ THIS BOOK?

Words and vocabulary are much more than just a piece of the educational jigsaw; words are a constant. Since the beginning of humankind, language and words have evolved with us and are the lifeblood of humanity. Vocabulary surrounds, engulfs and guides us every day; without words, we'd be lost. They are the subconscious map that guides us though day-to-day life, helping us to navigate the physical world we live in. It's something we don't think about – it's natural. Even now, reading this book, you're taking it for granted. Actually, words are a privilege. Without words, we would sadly be without enchanting literature, vital historical records, uniquely vibrant and diverse languages, loving conversations, mythical stories and inspirational song lyrics. Words are truly magical: they connect us at a deeper level. What would life be without words?

Grasshopper! Welcome and congratulations on beginning your epic journey towards becoming a Vocabulary Ninja Grand Master. At the simplest level, being a Vocabulary Ninja is about making words a priority in your classroom, empowering your pupils, having fun and enriching your whole school. Right from the outset though, it's important to understand that it starts with you. You have to be the leader, the modeller, the fun-maker, the person who makes mistakes and revels in it, the exemplar and the advocate. You have to be the Vocabulary Ninja for your pupils, and they will become your Grasshoppers. By 'mastering vocabulary' with Vocabulary Ninja, you will be igniting every area of your curriculum and be developing more independent and confident learners, as well as developing yourself.

As with anything that is worthwhile doing or that is to have any significant impact, it will take time. A marginal gains mentality is required. By keenly focusing on all of the smaller parts – 0.5 per cent here and 0.7 per cent there – we can slowly start to improve progress, standards and outcomes for all learners. To truly master vocabulary, we need to look at every aspect of learning and understand that all of the small parts will eventually add up to something really special. While walking along the corridor, how you speak to pupils and adults, at lunchtimes, greeting pupils, assemblies and in lessons – every aspect is hugely important. You have to become a Vocabulary NInja. One who Is ready to pounce on every opportunity throughout the whole school day, not just in an English lesson starter. (That wouldn't be ninja!) We will talk about marginal gains and micro-ambitions in greater detail in later chapters, and about how we can begin to be micro-successful.

The purpose of this book is to open your eyes to the power that words have, both inside and outside the classroom. A learner's understanding, knowledge and control of vocabulary have the power to unlock these learning doors and open them wide. Sadly, for many pupils, these learning doors can remain locked shut, rusted at the hinges, and vocabulary begins to become a significant barrier not just to learning, but to social interactions, communication, self-esteem, mental health and much more. Let's not allow vocabulary to be a subconscious element of your classroom that passes everyone by. Vocabulary must be at the conscious forefront, the frontline force of every conversation, every lesson, and every interaction in your school and classroom.

> **NINJA REFLECTIONS**
>
> This resource will provide you with a plethora of evidence, practical strategies, engaging games, resources and advice on how to bring words to life in your classroom and open up the doors to a world of understanding. It's one decision you will never regret!

## TAKING RESPONSIBILITY FOR VOCABULARY LEARNING

Imagine this scenario: a pupil comes into your lesson wanting to learn but doesn't understand a word or two. Not a huge problem, right? Well, just think of yourself in a meeting or professional development session. The person speaking is using a range of vocabulary that you are unfamiliar with. We've all been there – it's frustrating and you can feel like the session is passing you by so you just switch off altogether. And you're an educated adult. Now go back to the pupil. This pupil might encounter this same scenario every single lesson, every day – being switched off in a significant number of lessons because of previous experiences and the fact that vocabulary is a constant barrier. Still not a huge problem? Wrong. Most certainly you will be able to think of a pupil you are teaching or have taught for whom this is true. This is a real problem, and it's getting worse. As educators, we need to investigate the root causes of barriers to learning and try to unpick them; vocabulary, and a lack of it, has the power to slam the learning doors closed – permanently.

All of the blame for poor vocabulary cannot be put solely at the doorstep of the learner (a child). Yes, here it comes: we are just as culpable. How often have you started to teach a lesson, used a worksheet, read a text or put a test in front of a pupil and the barrier to them being successful in the given task isn't their mathematical or scientific knowledge, but the vocabulary, whether it be in the questions or the task itself? What makes this even worse in a lot of cases is that this cycle just repeats and repeats. Think about how demoralising this must be and imagine how you would feel. You can easily empathise and realise how quickly a learner could be switched off and demoralised. This child's progress in learning and negative behaviour traits can become serious issues. Think about pupils whose vocabulary has been neglected for years – for their whole life. We can all think of these pupils. Think of all of the time that is invested in managing or trying to transform their behaviour, with ultimately no real impact. Maybe we need to rethink where we invest our attentions and rethink what we value and prioritise. In fact, there's no 'maybe' about it – we *must* rethink how we approach vocabulary.

### READING FOR WRITING

If we think about some of our more successful learners, a broad generalisation would suggest they are competent readers. We always talk about how our successful writers are readers. 'You can tell they are a reader,' teachers say. But, if we think about this in more detail, how does reading transcend all other areas of learning? Well, quite simply, our more successful writers read more often, read more advanced texts than their peers, have conversations about reading and the words they encounter, and so have a vast repertoire of vocabulary that they understand and can actively draw upon. An analogy might look a little like this: there are two horses in a race over a mile. Let's call the race the 'Vocabulary Stakes'. One horse has 40 fences to hurdle along the way, the other has none.

In reality, the race is a lesson, learning and understanding are what's at stake and the handicap is vocabulary. Who's going to win? With the 'stakes' so high, can we afford for the race to be a handicap? The analogy is a sad one because it depicts learners as lone runners. We need to ensure that we act so that our learning race is run together, 'obstacle course' style. We know it's going to get dirty, there'll be a few scraped knees along the way, but regardless of how strong each individual is, some of the obstacles would be insurmountable alone. We will only be successful together.

As educators, we need to evaluate how we prepare and facilitate our learners for this learning race and plan to minimise the hurdles that they have to encounter. The first step is acknowledging that vocabulary does create a huge barrier and that we need to do something about it. Having an obstacle course mentality is another great analogy to apply to our mindset as educators, as we start to think about how we will go about making vocabulary a core focus within our classrooms. The barriers that we will face as educators will be constant and varied; there is no shortcut, no quick fix and no hack. Once we accept this, we can be better prepared to rise to the challenge on a day-to-day, lesson-by-lesson and minute-by-minute basis.

### ASPIRE TO INSPIRE

This book will equip you with the basics by providing you with a huge arsenal of practical ideas, lessons, games, resources, strategies and content to start your vocabulary journey in school and, if I dare say it, without getting bogged down in too much theory (just a sprinkling will do). It would be quite easy to talk about vocabulary being a huge barrier to understanding for pupils and then not apply it to this book for you as a reader. This book isn't going to baffle you with big words and challenging theories, as vocabulary might do for pupils in the classroom. I won't apologise for this simplistic approach – I don't intend on becoming a hypocrite. Vocabulary Ninja simply aspires to inspire other teaching practitioners to make vocabulary a priority that underpins all other teaching. As a full-time teacher myself, I know firsthand the significant impact that immersing learners in a vocabulary-oriented environment can have!

# VOCABULARY NINJA
# ROLE ON THE WALL

The Vocabulary Ninja Role on the wall poster (page 12) is your visual guide to the content found throughout this book. More importantly, the Vocabulary Ninja Role on the wall poster is a reference point for your own journey to becoming more Vocabulary Ninja and the type of mentality that you will have to adopt. It is also a reminder that, even on the toughest of days, you are awesome and you got this! By being more aware of your own state of mind and the external influences that can impact upon it, you can be better prepared to be even more awesome every day, and not sweat the small stuff. Even by coming this far, I know you are ready to make every day better for yourself and your pupils!

As with a traditional role on the wall activity, the words outside the ninja allude to the external, social, cultural and environmental factors that you will need to consider and understand as you progress through your journey of enlightenment.

The interior of the ninja is less cluttered, more orderly and focused. This is exactly how we need to be, as teachers. On the outside we have external factors that will constantly fluctuate in frequency and intensity, whereas we have a greater degree of control of our thoughts and attitudes towards the day's teaching and vocabulary.

All of the factors identified on the Vocabulary Ninja Role on the wall poster impact on your overall effectiveness and your overall awesomeness. A better understanding of each factor and its potential impact will allow you to be more ninja each and every day!

# VOCABULARY NINJA ROLE ON THE WALL
## THE NINJA MENTALITY

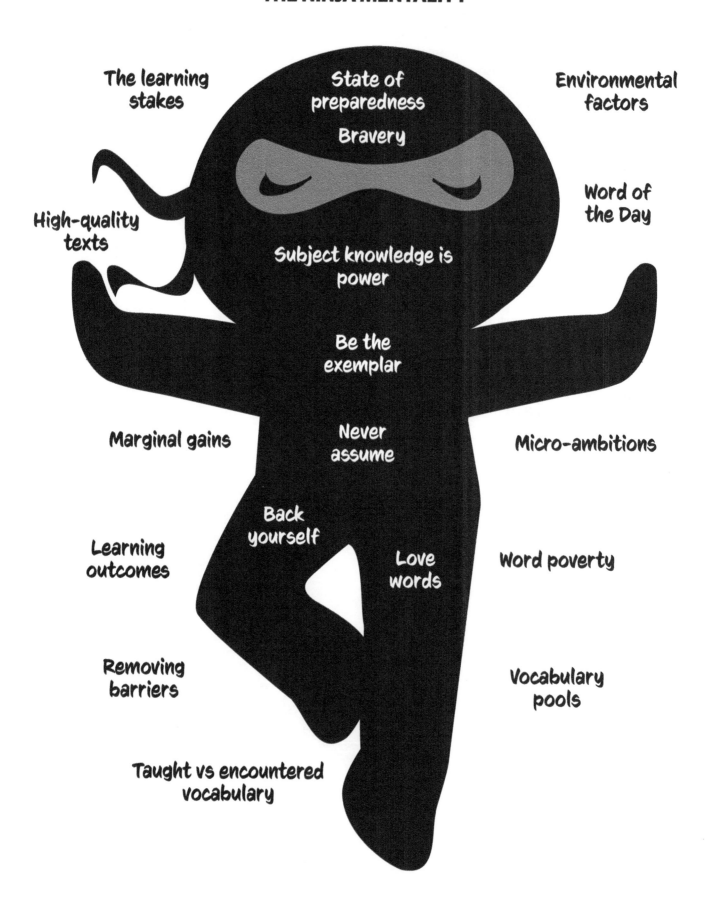

# 2 – PROBLEMS, SOLUTIONS AND BEING A VOCABULARY NINJA

This chapter explores some of the reasons why pupils' vocabularies might be limited and what the impact of this could be. The chapter also promotes the importance of developing your own 'Vocabulary Ninja' teaching mentality as the first step towards effectively bringing vocabulary to life in your classroom.

> These are the mere ramblings of a Vocabulary Ninja; my pearls of wisdom, advice and spiritual guidance. Beyond all of this, the chapter aims to provoke you. Provoke you into thinking about yourself, your ambitions, your context and your pupils. Even more, I want to provoke you into challenging yourself to be that little bit better, that little bit more ninja.

## VOCABULARY ISN'T A LESSON, IT'S LIFE

Before we discuss the problem, let's look at the solution: **vocabulary isn't a lesson, it's life**. We can't think about timetabling it or giving it a slot in which it can be observed. Due to the hectic nature of teaching, we find a strange comfort in being able to box something up, put it in a slot, so that we can tick it off, say it's done, forget about it for today. The safety net has been cast…

So, the solution. The solution is valuing every interaction, every conversation, every minute, every hour, every lesson and every day. Each smaller moment enhances the next. If we value all of the smaller parts of learning, the larger parts will take care of themselves. This may be a little corny, but when I talk about being a 'Vocabulary Ninja' this is what I mean: being present in each and every moment as a class teacher and understanding that vocabulary and language are constants, that they permeate every aspect of life, both in and out of school. Being present is one thing, but we must be vigilant and ready to act, model, prepare, discuss, correct, celebrate, joke and inspire, too. There is simply no way that we can compartmentalise it, contain it, box it up, timetable it, say 'it's done'. You have to be ready to pounce on every opportunity. And believe me, there will be lots of opportunities, because there are lots of words!

## BECOME A VOCABULARY GRAND MASTER

As a teacher myself, I used to find comfort in knowing something had been 'developed or produced' to meet the needs of a certain year; a word list for example, or a specific text and planned unit. As time passed, I found that this comfort blanket didn't really help me. Instead, it insulated me from that fear factor and gave me something to blame if things didn't go quite right. By fear factor, bluntly, I mean that such subject packs insulated me from poor levels of subject knowledge, my area of weakness. Actually, I just needed to take responsibility and become better at what I did.

I needed to understand words in much more detail because they made up every aspect of what I taught – the grammar, the etymology, the conventions, the terminology, and everything to do with it. I had to make myself a better teacher before I stood a chance of developing more successful and confident pupils. This is still true today. Each day I try to be micro-ambitious and aim to be marginally better by the end of it.

## WORD DEPRIVATION

From a solution to a problem. What is 'word deprivation'? Quite simply, word deprivation is a lack of words that a learner can draw upon in written and oral communication. In other words, they have a limited vocabulary. On the other hand, pupils with more expansive and broad repertoires of words could be thought of as being 'word-rich'. Alex Quigley, author of *Closing the Vocabulary Gap*, refers to this concept as pupils being 'word-wealthy', whereby pupils need to develop a vocabulary of 50,000 words if they are statistically likely to be successful in education and beyond. This is a huge undertaking when you consider that 'average' pupils learn 2,000–3,000 words a year in education. Whichever way you look at it, the curriculum alone and general teaching is not sufficient for most pupils to reach this magical figure for working vocabulary. Let's not forget, these are the figures for the average pupil. What about those pupils who have other significant barriers to learning – pupil premium, special educational needs, socially mobile, English as an additional language, and so on? You can see how, quite quickly, a large number of pupils are likely to be word deprived – literally starved of words, faced with a lexical famine.

If pupils don't understand enough words (not the elaborate and fancy words – I mean the ones we take for granted and assume that pupils know), how can we expect them to engage at any level within the classroom? Let's think back to how vocabulary can be a barrier to learning. For some pupils, even in the early stages of school, the barriers are huge and sadly often misunderstood. Educators may spot that there is an issue, but a pupil's working lexical level probably isn't the first thing most educators will think about investigating. Thus, the curriculum moves on and the barrier becomes bigger and harder to overcome. Yes, this won't always be the case for certain pupils; some children have additional barriers that impact on learning. But if we focus on the majority of pupils, we can ensure that pupils are actively expanding their vocabularies, making regular deposits into their 'word bank' and becoming word-hungry, rather than starved of words. This is our responsibility and one that, if we can tackle it, will have far-reaching effects – across subjects, schools and all pupils' journey in life.

# THE NATIONAL CURRICULUM

The National Curriculum lists 100 spellings for Years 5 and 6. Two whole years of learning, restricted to 100 'essential' words that are found as requirements for national writing expectations, display boards and beyond. There are millions of words for us to explore, so why do we restrict ourselves? We have to aspire to be better, more adventurous and drag ourselves away from this safety net approach to words and vocabulary.

The Oxford Living Dictionaries estimates there are somewhere in the region of three quarters of a million words in the English language and, as stated earlier, pupils require a working vocabulary of 50,000 words. Yet somehow we are happy to accept that just 100 of those words are a vital component of two whole years of school. I find this hard to accept or endorse. It's a huge contradiction and one that we must be aware of for the best interests of our pupils. Now, let's be clear: I am not trying to rain down some form of anarchistic vocabulary-based rebellion against the National Curriculum. Far from it. But deciding that only 0.013 per cent of all the possible words available to us should be deemed an essential focus over two years just seems insane. Let's bring in another analogy. Let's compare our 'word diet' with an actual diet: if you were to consume only 0.013 per cent of the available food sources over a two-year period, regardless of what they were, you would most likely be in a state of great ill health, dangerously malnourished or, most likely, not here to read this fabulous book. You would have been deprived of the crucial vitamins, minerals, proteins and nutrients of a balanced diet that are essential for good health. Well, the same applies if we want to be 'word healthy'. We need to consume a balanced diet of words from a range of sources and contexts:

- high-quality texts
- conversation
- independent reading
- being read to
- modelled writing
- listening to others
- non-fiction and fiction
- poetry
- direct teaching
- books
- picture books
- assemblies
- trips and experts
- break times
- performances.

This isn't an exhaustive list either – the opportunities are endless; words and language can be drawn from anywhere. If we are to promote more creative, inquisitive and independent learners, we need to be a little bit more, well, ninja, and pounce on every one of the opportunities listed above. This will ultimately help make children better readers, writers and communicators.

## ARE TEACHERS THE PROBLEM?

So, hopefully we agree that we need an enriched diet of language. But, are teachers one of the problems when it comes to word deprivation? I think I was, so maybe we are. Due to the complex nature of teaching, it would be fair to moot that vocabulary is something that we hope happens. For some of us, thinking about the nuts and bolts of words and language is just something that we don't have time for, or don't realise the importance of. Teaching is undoubtedly one of the most rewarding, yet challenging, professions; some of us even see teaching as our *raison d'être*, or 'reason for being'. Even the process of becoming a teacher, whichever route taken, involves late nights, early mornings, blood, sweat and tears, and the unpredictable on a daily basis. We are so exhaustingly busy, working in this high-pressure environment that the system creates, that it is easy to lose focus on what's important. My point is that words are what are important, and that we have potentially lost sight of this fundamental fact. Words can be the biggest barriers to learning for pupils but are also the most powerful weapons we can hope to equip them with.

Let's refocus and think about 'word deprivation'. If our pupils have a limited understanding of words, then

Vocabulary Ninja © Andrew Jennings, 2024

pronouncing, reading, writing, sharing, choosing and playing with words all become increasingly difficult. These basic skills that begin in Reception become barriers to learning because words help to form nearly every aspect of the curriculum a child is exposed to, in some way, shape or form. Yet, I think pupils, ECTs and experienced teachers alike have been done a huge disservice, for a long time, in being made to believe that words, vocabulary and language will just be learnt and understood on their own. Again, we come back to a safety net approach to teaching, where security for teachers is found in word banks, lists, schemes and being told what to do so that we don't get 'in trouble'. And this is understandable – believe me, I get it – but we need to just get over this and start to be braver.

> We must start to think for ourselves, be brave, make decisions, be passionate and get excited. Be more ninja. I understand that your school will have systems and processes that teachers will need to adhere to, but within all of that noise, you just have to find your inner Vocabulary Ninja.

## USING THE IDEAS IN THIS BOOK

As discussed earlier, being a little bit more ninja doesn't mean you are going to begin to teach your own rebellious curriculum. It means you are going to increase the value of every idle opportunity or lazy expression that the day offers up.

Let's begin by looking at a typical day. You have a guided reading session to teach first, then have to lead an assembly before introducing a new mathematical concept and, in English, you must edit those final drafts just before lunch. This will involve devouring a quick sandwich as you set up for PE and resource your geography lesson for last period. Oh, and you're on break duty too. Your TA is off sick and the office staff have kindly informed you that the photocopier is broken. Awesome!

Within all of this mayhem that is teaching, your ninja mentality and focus on vocabulary is vital. What is it that's important? As you can already see, there is no extra time in your day to dedicate to vocabulary. Vocabulary and words will encompass all of these events and the pockets of time within and between every lesson. This is where you will make the difference; this is where you need to go it alone and take control.

There is a level of genuine and pure exhilaration that comes from taking control – believe me, it's great.

Yes, undoubtedly mistakes will be made, but at least they are yours; at least you can feel an emotion, such as regret. Even in experiencing regret, there is still satisfaction in knowing that you *tried*. I don't really think anyone has ever really learned from someone else's mistakes. You have to experience it yourself. What makes it yet more powerful is when you quickly start to reap the rewards, as you will when your pupils begin to use this language in conversations and in their writing.

To begin with, it's quite simply all about having the right mentality.

## THREE MANTRAS

Mantras can often offer up insights into the type of mindset we are trying to adopt. Again, this isn't about rebellion; it's about belief and positivity – you can do it; you are amazing. Here are three mantras that Vocabulary Ninja loves, all with varying levels of formality – but nonetheless powerful and apt. Plus, every ninja needs a mantra – it's a ninja thing.

### 'YOU GOTTA BACK YOURSELF!'

Certainly the most informal example of the three, but it's great. 'You gotta back yourself!' is so true. Everything in the last five to six paragraphs could have just been edited out and this mantra put in its place. Sport has messages and principles that adapt extremely easily into education – marginal gains, for example. For me, 'you gotta back yourself' was a mantra that came to life while studying and playing sport competitively at the University of Hull. It was often used in jest between myself and housemates, Mr Sims, Mr Rodley, Mr Grant, Mr Jackson and Mr Kench (whose names I use so formally as all are now teachers too, not the cast list of Reservoir Dogs!). You have to back yourself. The classroom is your domain, so make decisions and see them through, reflect and go again.

### 'IT'S BETTER TO ASK FOR FORGIVENESS THAN TO ASK FOR PERMISSION'

The next mantra is most likely a headteacher's worst nightmare come to fruition, but let's not worry about that too much. Believe in yourself – if you have an idea, it's probably a good one, so go for it. Sometimes there is a level of security in asking for permission. It absolves you of responsibility. You are far more likely to invest yourself in something if it is your idea, your project, and if you are personally invested in the outcomes. This is a great position to be in. I'm not for one minute suggesting you all of a sudden take a group of children on an unannounced trip to your nearest dangerous place. No. I want you to think about your classroom, corridors, nooks, crannies, spaces, unused equipment, facilities, routines, and so on. Be creative and forward-thinking. Be inventive. Tear down that display; take apart a monitor; do the latest trending edu-idea; be passionate. Just do it! You, your pupils and your school will reap the rewards.

Unless we are prepared to take control of our classroom, our own practice and what we prioritise, then (as a famous film once said), resistance is futile. Once you have the right mindset, you can begin your own journey towards developing yourself, driving your CPD in the direction you want it to be driven, and knowing that you are making decisions for you and your learners!

### 'DON'T CELEBRATE TOO PROFUSELY IN VICTORY OR BERATE YOURSELF TOO MUCH IN DEFEAT'

The final mantra that resonates from personal experiences throughout my time in education is this: 'don't celebrate too profusely in victory or berate yourself too much in defeat'. Victory and defeat could also be reworded as highs and lows, or ups and downs. The essence of this mantra is all about maintaining a grasp on level-headedness or perspective. No matter how good you think you are, you can get better, and if things seem bad, they're probably not as bad as you think. The parallels to sport are easy to see once again. Listen to any professional sportsperson or team interviewed after a euphoric win or demoralising defeat. In that moment, they will be overjoyed with happiness or overcome with grief, but it is the most successful among them who manage to move on very quickly and learn from what has taken place – whether it was positive or negative. Yes, celebrate, or be disappointed, but learn quickly and move on. Tomorrow is another day to strive to improve from where we are now.

# VOCABULARY AND YOU

So, what do mentalities and mantras have to do with mastering vocabulary? Well, everything really. Just as they have everything to do with education and everything to do with you. There is never one without the other; each is a vital component, reliant on the other. We all have good and bad days, and the same can be said for lessons, conversations, lesson plans, observations, or even whole years. Part of my own journey in understanding the importance of vocabulary was more of a journey in understanding myself, not listening to too many external influences, and doing each day on my terms. So, in one sense, it was more like a journey to believing in myself rather than just believing in vocabulary. Vocabulary became my unwitting partner and passion!

Once again, we must bring ourselves back to word deprivation. Without making words a priority, the children in your class will always be deprived of words or be falling well short of the magical 50,000. Prioritising words will open up the doors to a whole new world of understanding for you and your pupils. You need to be your class's Vocabulary Ninja. You need to back yourself. You may need to ask for forgiveness, in victory or defeat, but be content in knowing that you will have made a much bigger difference than you can ever comprehend.

## THE MOST PRECIOUS COMMODITY

The world is forever changing, becoming smaller, and at an exponential rate over the last 20 years due to technology, politics, economics and social norms changing beyond recognition. It's hard to keep up. The world is a very fast-moving place now for young people to be; technology has rapidly become virtually indispensable for everyone. Video games, smartphones, apps, social media, virtual reality and television are developed and consumed at a mind-boggling rate. There are so many fabulous innovations and advances that make the world a more exciting place to live. All the while, people and families are becoming increasingly busy, and even with all of these technological conveniences, time is still the most precious commodity. And that is why what you do with your pupils during the short time you spend with them is critical.

For just a moment, let's forget financial poverty and political climates, and think carefully about our pupils living in 'word poverty'. When we think about word poverty, it's important to think about *all* pupils, not just pupils who may be living in actual poverty. Word poverty is all about time and exposure. How much of our pupils' time involves exposure to high-quality language, words and vocabulary? Pupils will always spend significantly more time at home or in environments other than school. It's during these times that individual experiences and exposure to language will vary dramatically. Some pupils will read daily, be read to and have diverse conversations filled with expressive language with adults who have robust vocabularies of their own. Lots of children won't have this experience.

The pupils in your care might only be exposed to your enriched environment for 30 of 168 hours in a week. That's only 17 per cent of every week that is spent in a language-rich and hopefully word-wealthy environment where words are celebrated, played with and valued. Take away break times, lunchtimes, assemblies, days off and trips, and it's probably closer to 15 per cent of every week. Each year, of the 8,760 hours in that year, it's likely that a pupil will spend no more than 1,140 hours with you – that's 13 per cent of that whole year! Why not break it down even further? Of those six hours in school each day, if you only ever focused on words for an English or reading lesson, let's say five hours a week for example, you would only be actively engaging in 'language' for three per cent of a seven-day week or two per cent of every year, which, scarily enough, only equates to 55.1 school days spent focusing on 'language' during a pupil's time from Reception to Year 6.

> **Make time for vocabulary each day. Just five to 15 minutes. You won't regret it.**
>
> NINJA NOTES

We can't create more time, and the curriculum is demanding. Go back to the principles of being a Vocabulary Ninja. Every interaction, every conversation, every minute, every lesson, every day is vital – it's about the sum of all the small parts and valuing the marginal gains of each interaction, taking pride in the micro-victories and evaluating your micro-defeats. We have to make the most of the time that pupils are with us in school.

What is mind blowing about numbers like these is that, considering how little time might actually be spent on 'language' in the grand scheme of things, you do an amazing job in the short space of time that you do actually have with your pupils. Vivid and heart-breaking narratives, emotive poetry, captivating diary entries and forensic non-fiction reports – it's all magnificent.

Some pupils, in fact a large proportion of pupils, will spend a much larger percentage of time doing things other than being exposed to high-quality language. And believe it or not, this is OK. We want children to live exciting lives out in the world, kicking balls, climbing trees, gaming, having sleepovers, and so on. But, not everyone lives in this idealistic land of childhood.

This raises two very important issues to be aware of. One is that the time that pupils spend with you in school is extremely precious, more valuable than you may have realised. Every interaction, every conversation, every minute, every hour, every day is incalculably valuable. Secondly, language and vocabulary must be at the centre of everything that we do in every aspect of the school day; confining it to a single lesson just isn't good enough.

## 'THE ANIMALS WHO USE THE POND DON'T JUST DRINK FROM IT'

You know better than most that, depending on their context, some of your pupils will be exposed to some pretty terrible vocabulary on a daily basis. The word pool that they swim in every day is extremely shallow, it doesn't rain very often and lots of the animals who use the pond don't just drink from it. People will generally only use the vocabulary that their environment demands of them, meaning that the interactions your pupils have on a daily basis – the people who surround them, the jobs their parents do, and so on – directly affect the vocabulary they will subconsciously use. Your job is to begin to make this a conscious process. As alluded to earlier, the time spent with you is indescribably valuable.

You need to bring the rain! Not in the military sense, but in the climatological sense. You need to be the cumulonimbus cloud that pours down onto your pupils' shallow word pool, making it a little deeper in each moment and understanding that every raindrop matters. Even now, I'm especially careful not to say *each* day, and I'll say it once again – *every* interaction, *every* conversation, *every* minute, *every* hour will make up every day. Thinking about each day is too big; it isn't micro-ambitious enough, it allows for gaps, missed opportunities. If we are micro-ambitious enough and understand the importance of every raindrop, we will begin to turn our shallow vocabulary puddles into vast reservoirs of language.

# BECOMING A VOCABULARY NINJA

Anecdotes, metaphors, myths and analogies aside, I can only presume that you would like to know a little more about the impact vocabulary can have within the classroom and why you should be a Vocabulary Ninja.

As stated earlier, vocabulary cuts across all aspects of your curriculum. Being micro-ambitious with vocabulary and focusing at a word level can have a profound effect on pupils' writing. The great thing about vocabulary is that it is extremely accessible for all pupils – it literally empowers them, they can control it and it's theirs. By bringing vocabulary to the forefront of your teaching, using the strategies identified in this book, you will quickly begin to improve writing standards across the curriculum because of the wider vocabulary and increased understanding of pupils. Pupils will quickly become adept at using more complex language, varying verbs and adjectives, while developing a greater capacity to show and not tell (offering inference via vocabulary to the audience). Quite quickly, 'big' will become 'enormous'; 'happy' will become 'elated'; and what was once 'boring' will become 'mundane', even 'tedious'. Repetition of language will reduce and pupils' shallow word pools will have become a little deeper.

A word of warning: as with all learning, not all pupils will necessarily be ready to work at the same word level. Success, progress, achievement – whatever you want to call it – will present itself in very different ways for different pupils. You should value and celebrate them equally. This phrase perfectly encapsulates this sentiment: 'One child's "huge" is another child's "voracious."' (Jack Phillips, @Mr_P_Hillips, describing two very different pupils, both increasing their word pool depth and becoming increasingly word wealthy.) Both word choices are just as fantastic and wonderful as the other. They are both filled with authorial intent, unique voices and an empowered independence. The impact of vocabulary on pupil writing is potentially endless, only limited by the words they are limited to. (I just blew my own mind!)

## A WORD ABOUT GRAMMAR

A word-level focus within writing also offers perpetual opportunities to embed discussion linked to the basics of grammar. Every word has a job. Within every sentence, each word is performing a role and, as you know, some words are rather versatile and can perform many different jobs. Grammar is another area where you find the teaching safety net, mostly because of a 'requires improvement' level of subject knowledge. The teaching of grammar becomes an endless list of clichés or phrases that are competently repeated by pupils. You know the ones: 'adjectives are describing words', 'verbs are doing words' and 'a noun is a person place or a thing'. You hear these safety net phrases all of the time – we find comfort in them. I used to say them regularly, mostly because I wasn't confident in my subject knowledge or even with the basics of grammar. The problem with all of these phrases is that they are all superficial. There is no depth of knowledge or understanding for either the teacher or the learner. It's all just smoke and mirrors!

The scenario probably goes a little like this: during an English observation, grammar inevitably crops up. With the observer hovering closely over your shoulder or while keenly inspecting your displays, you are busy working with Jimmy and his table of typical pupils. You are helping them develop a descriptive passage about an engaging Literacy Shed video. You decide that adding some adjectives is the next step (as per the plan). You ask the table, 'Who can give me an adjective to make this sentence a little more impressive?', only to be greeted by blank expressions (not per the plan).

In your head, you are furious: 'I can't believe they are doing this to me! We did it yesterday! Aaargggghhhh!' You wisely decide to widen the discussion. You offer up the usual question, 'Can somebody tell me what an adjective is?' Hands from the usual suspects rise and the inevitable answer will come, 'It's a describing word.' You graciously accept the answer, with a nod to the observer and move on, satisfied that you have demonstrated your subject knowledge, even though your focus group and the wider class is probably still none the wiser.

In order for grammatical understanding to improve for teacher and learners, we must begin to develop a more open culture where each new word offers an opportunity for grammatical discussion. We need to be more forensic in our approach to each word that we encounter. The brilliant thing about discussing grammar while discussing words is that it offers up context, making any discussions and learning more memorable. Some of the most memorable contexts will undoubtedly come from the books that you are reading in class. This is why exposure to high-quality literature is so important. Subsequent chapters will provide glossaries, agreed terminology, activities and strategies to improve the teaching and learning of grammar in your classroom.

## WHERE TO FIND INSPIRATION AND SUPPORT

Literacy, reading, writing, grammar, spelling and vocabulary are all inextricably (awesome word meaning 'impossible to disentangle or separate') linked – no one area is more important than any other; the success of one stems from another. Developing your ninja mentality and a forensic classroom culture are essential if your pupils are to learn. Your journey towards a ninja mentality and forensic classroom culture will allow you to be fully engaged with every learning moment that words present.

Ultimately, I want to convince you that making vocabulary a priority is worthwhile and to provoke you into thinking about how you can improve. Undoubtedly there will be significant barriers. Will those barriers go away? Probably not. So it will be tough, that's for sure. Definitely use research to support what you do, seek the support of other professionals, and read a journal or become active on social media.

# 3 – THE VALUE OF VOCABULARY

Vocabulary Ninja's core mantra continues to be 'Teaching Simplified, Learning Amplified': the aim is to simplify any teaching processes, while amplifying the outcomes for learners. With a huge amount of literature available on the subject of children's vocabulary, it's important to be able to focus on what's relevant to the primary classroom and, more importantly, how it can be implemented consistently across a whole school.

An important study on children's vocabulary, language and communication is Hart and Risley (2003). Made up of 42 families with children from seven months to three years old, from varying socio-economic backgrounds (see diagram below), the study investigated the impact of the home environment on children's early development.

**The number of words per hour (WPH) heard by children of different socio-economic backgrounds (Hart and Risley, 2003)**

The study's findings uncovered the significant impact that a child's home life – in terms of the adults and environments that they are exposed to in their early years – can have on their vocabulary development. Most significantly, the study highlighted that in the first four years of life, children from the lowest income backgrounds will hear fewer than a third of the words that children from the highest income families would, resulting in a word gap of approximately 30 million words.

This gap only grows in the subsequent years. While the progress in learning of children from the poorest backgrounds is inhibited, progress is accelerated for children from higher income backgrounds. The study found:

- Eighty-six to ninety-eight per cent of the words used at age three were derived from the caregiver. The words, speech patterns and conversation duration and skill were nearly identical to that of the caregiver.

- On average, children from the lowest income caregivers heard 125,000 more words of discouragement compared to the 560,000 more words of encouragement that children of high-income caregivers were exposed to.

The study followed up with two-thirds of the families years later and reported how the children's vocabularies at age three were highly indicative of academic performance at age 10 and 11.

The picture painted could be considered rather bleak, especially for the families and children who find themselves further down the socio-economic spectrum.

Fortunately, we have an opportunity that presents itself as the solution to our vocabulary problem… school! School, for all pupils, provides a magical opportunity to create a fifth socio-economic bubble, irrespective of wealth. A bubble that is filled with vocabulary, language and communication 'caregivers' and a safe, stimulating environment. Regardless of a child's socio-economic background, this magical moment occurs every day. They come to school, with you! Their 'caregiver' of vocabulary, language and communication!

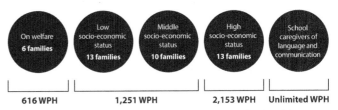

**School caregivers have the potential to offer limitless words per hour**

The word 'caregiver' must become central to our own approach to creating a vocabulary-rich environment for our learners. If we think about Hart and Risley (2003), the 'caregiver' is the central factor that determines the quality of communication a child is exposed to. Once in our care, we are responsible for the development of the children's vocabulary, language and communication skills.

As teachers, we must look at the findings of such a study and think about how this directly relates to our role as 'caregiver' and how the environment we provide for the children will significantly impact their learning.

# 4 – TIERS OF VOCABULARY

The 'Tiers of Vocabulary' model was first developed by Beck, McKeown and Kucan in their 2013 book *Bringing Words to Life*. It helps by breaking vocabulary down into three distinct tiers and can be used as a framework for developing children's writing.

This framework can be easily used in any classroom to help think about where and when we might focus on and teach the different types of vocabulary that all of our pupils will benefit from.

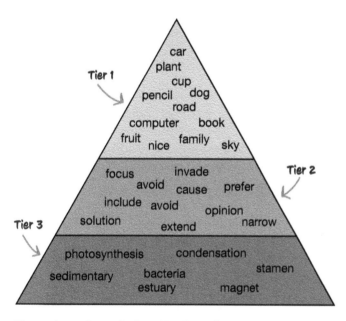

**Three tiers of vocabulary (Beck et al., 2013)**

Let's take a closer look at the different tiers of vocabulary so that we might better understand each one and the impact it can have on our classrooms.

## TIER 1 VOCABULARY

Tier 1 vocabulary generally requires no formal teaching and consists of words learned through daily interactions. It is centrally important to Hart and Risley's (2003) findings, as it is made up of children's foundational vocabulary which can be dependent on their parents and socio-economic background.

Tier 1 vocabulary is the foundation of a child's ability to communicate in both oral and written forms. The depth of this foundation depends largely on their caregivers and the social environment at home.

## Five strategies to develop Tier 1 vocabulary

Strategies like these can help to actively develop children's Tier 1 vocabulary in school, without creating any additional workload.

**1 Prioritise time for reading aloud**

Plan daily read-aloud sessions where you read engaging and age-appropriate books to your students. Pause at intervals to discuss the meanings of unfamiliar words and encourage children to ask questions about the story. Simple, but very effective!

**2 Activate conversations**

Having conversations with children is very important, especially for those moving into Year 1 and Year 2. See Early vocabulary development in the EYFS (page 24).

**3 Word/picture wall**

Create interactive word walls in the classroom by displaying common Tier 1 words. You could also include words encountered in the stories that have been read aloud. Use corresponding pictures, which children could create themselves, and use the words in sentences to help children understand their meanings in context.

**4 Contextual learning**

Relate new words to real-life situations and experiences. For example, during a nature walk, discuss the names of plants, animals and natural features. This helps children connect words to their surroundings and reinforces their understanding.

**5 'Ask me about' stickers**

Make sure all adults in school are aware of what this sticker means when they see a child wearing one. Use a typical sticky label that says 'Ask me about…' and then something related to that pupil's learning or achievements. For example, 'Ask me about my football game at the weekend' or 'Ask me about the book I'm reading'. Something that, as the teacher, you know the pupil can discuss. Specifically target pupils who you know have underdeveloped vocabularies. Before you know it, this pupil will be having constant conversations with adults around school!

# TIER 2 VOCABULARY

Tier 2 vocabulary are words that are high frequency (occur regularly in all text types), cross-curricular (make links between subjects) and essential for widening knowledge and understanding. Rather important then!

Tier 2 vocabulary must be explicitly taught to pupils, to ensure that they understand it properly and have opportunities to apply this new learning. *Vocabulary Ninja* aims to focus on Tier 2 vocabulary for the Word of the Day, to ensure that each day, a specific Tier 2 piece of vocabulary is being taught on its own merit, but also with the knowledge that the word adds value within the school curriculum and content. Ideally, we want to teach pupils Tier 2 vocabulary that is drawn from the text, video, model text or other stimulus we are using to drive children's writing in school. This is because this vocabulary has instant applications within this immediate context, but due to its high-frequency and cross-curricular nature, the likelihood is that this word will arise again and again. Understanding such words then allows children to independently access texts and articulate themselves more accurately as authors.

Ideally via a Word of the Day, we should be aiming to teach a new Tier 2 word each day. So, let's explore the value of Tier 2 words and try to understand why we need to teach them.

For example, we might choose to teach the word '**invade**'. Now, when teaching the book *Friend or Foe* by Michael Morpurgo, I know that the word 'invade' or the concept of invasion occurs early on in the book. I also know that it is an important concept for the pupils to understand, not only from a reading point of view, but also for their writing at the end of the week.

Having chosen to teach the word **invade**, let's explore the value it represents.

**Value Link 1** – In teaching the meaning of an invasion, I would use the context of the book and World War Two, to present the concept of what 'invade/invasion' means. I'd explain that 'an invasion is when we have one country/person/entity/body/party who want to try and take control of another country/person/entity/body/party, who don't want this to happen, and so there is a conflict.' This is exactly what happens in a war, and in World War Two, this happened with Germany and other countries across the world. So, within a historical context, the children would understand. Within history, there are many other historical examples of war which their knowledge can also be linked to.

But the initial premise is central to unlocking understanding across other subject areas. Not just in the context of war, but what the word 'invade' or 'invasion' means. Look again at the definition:

'An invasion is when we have one country/person/entity/body/party who want to try and take control of another country/person/entity/body/party, who don't want this to happen, and so there is a conflict.'

The child's understanding of the concept is now much more concrete because of the Tier 2 piece of vocabulary. Without it, the concept and understanding are much more abstract and won't be retained.

**Value Link 2** – Imagine we are teaching a science lesson about bacteria and the human body.

As you read the science example below, try to be aware of what your brain does automatically. From your strong understanding of 'invade', your brain will naturally start to develop a picture of what's happening.

If children had no prior knowledge of this subject, but we stated this fact: 'Bacteria invade the human body,' they should easily be able to articulate what they think might be going on here, even though they have no previous knowledge.

'Bacteria want to try and take control of the body by invading it, but the human body doesn't want this to happen, and so there is a conflict.' From here, we could introduce the concept of white blood cells and the cellular conflict that occurs within the body, so children understand what is happening. But this knowledge is all activated by the Tier 2 vocabulary of 'invade'.

**Value Link 3** – General reading encounters. Children could very easily be reading a text about an 'invasive' species of wasp that is affecting the bumblebee. If a child was reading this text independently, then just understanding the word 'invade' or 'invasive' will allow them to develop a picture of what is happening and better understand what they are reading.

**Value Link 4** – ICT – Invasion of privacy! When introducing this concept in a computing lesson, the concept of invasion of personal details and passwords is very important. If children understand invasion they can confidently be introduced to the idea of invasion of privacy and make more links with a new subject area.

**Value Link 5** – PE – Invasion Games! Rugby, football, basketball, netball, hockey, and so on.

Quite simply, the central objective of many sports are invasion games, where teams must move into other teams' zones or areas of a pitch. Understanding the fact that such a game is an invasion game instantly highlights to the child what is likely to happen.

There are many more links to be made across the curriculum with such a word, and the value and importance of link scannot be understated! When Vocabulary Ninja says, 'Words unlock the doors to a world of understanding!', this is exactly what I mean.

## PAIRING BOOKS FOR A COMPOUND EFFECT!

Once words are taught, these words must be displayed in the classroom (see Chapter 8: The Vocabulary Environment – Your Classroom). Over a half term, try to pair books that have similar contexts, where the words drawn from one stimulus will support the learning and have a profound impact on the next. So, for example, in Year 6, I would pair *Friend or Foe* by Michael Morpurgo with *Rose Blanche* by Roberto Innocenti. I would further compound this by teaching a local history unit alongside these books, linked to the Bombardment of Hartlepool. These are three very similar contexts where all the vocabulary taught supports understanding in another areas and supports children making those links within their learning. Very powerful stuff!

# TIER 3 VOCABULARY

Tier 3 vocabulary is extremely low frequency (hardly ever crops up) and is very subject specific. So, for example, words like photosynthesis, evaporation, estuary and sedimentary. These words mean very specific things linked to a certain topic, like plants or rocks and soils, and will only arise when covering that topic. However, this doesn't mean that these words are not important; they still cover understanding, just in a very specific way. The words still need to be taught but they can only be taught as part of those topics and lessons and not as a Word of the Day.

When Tier 3 vocabulary arises in fiction, it may be important to explain what this vocabulary means in a precise way, otherwise key imagery or general understanding may be lost.

**Example 1** – When reading *The Wreck of the Zanzibar*, the word 'jib' is used a lot throughout the text. Essentially a 'jib' is a small vessel, a bit like a rowing boat. We couldn't choose this word as a Word of the Day teaching moment because it will be very unlikely that children will encounter this word again, but when encountered in the text, we should be telling them that this is a small wooden boat.

**Example 2** – Within the first chapter of *Room 13* by Robert Swindells, the word 'stalactite' is used in a dream sequence to describe how the blank paint had dried on a metal seagull and run, making the bird look more like a bat. For the imagery aspect, it's important that the children understand what a stalactite is and looks like: a rock formation that looks like an icicle. Again, we only want to spend 10 seconds ensuring the children understand what it is and then move on. In this instance, showing an image may provide complete clarity. The likelihood of 'stalactite' being encountered again is extremely low.

# 190 IS THE MAGIC NUMBER

So now we understand the problem, we can start to think more specifically around how we address the issue in school. We can also look at how the tiers of vocabulary can help us to focus in on what vocabulary to teach and when. We will then have the most significant impact on outcomes without making additional work for ourselves.

It would be fair to say that the 'vocabulary gap' is one that we will never close, but we must have a simple yet strategic plan that everyone in the school is aware of when it comes to the role that vocabulary plays in school. It should be a simple thread that weaves its way through both literacy and the school's wider curriculum – a living, breathing consciousness.

Well then! 190 is the magic number. But why? 190 represents the approximate number of days in an academic year. So, as a maximum, we only have 190 opportunities to explicitly teach a new word each day to our pupils. These 190 days essentially represent 190 words that we are going to teach.

So, if we have such a finite opportunity to teach new vocabulary, we must ensure that we are choosing the most valuable words. These should be words that are high frequency, likely to be encountered within our curriculum and that will allow pupils to make connections between knowledge.

Using Tiers 1, 2 and 3 vocabulary as a lens, we can start to focus in on which pieces of vocabulary we want to teach in those extremely valuable 190 days across the academic year.

## TIER 1 VOCABULARY

Via conversation, we want to prioritise and develop oral modelling, reading aloud, vocabulary displays and enhancement of environments. We may need to explicitly teach some Tier 1 vocabulary, especially when teaching pupils who have English as an Additional Language (EAL), Special Educational Needs and Disabilities (SEND) or are under the care of a Speech and Language Thearpy (SaLT) service.

## TIER 2 VOCABULARY

We need to teach these words daily and explicitly to ensure children have a comprehensive understanding of them. We will do this via the Word of the Day teaching process, ideally at the beginning of an English lesson. (See the 80 per cent rule below on how we should be approaching and choosing the right vocabulary to teach.) Remember, if we only have 190 precious opportunities to explicitly teach new vocabulary, we need to choose the most versatile and high-frequency words for the specific children we teach.

## TIER 3 VOCABULARY

This highly specific vocabulary should be taught in highly specific lessons. So, technical vocabulary linked to rocks and soil, such as *igneous*, *sedimentary* and *metamorphic*, should be taught within a rocks and soil topic. It is important for pupils to learn the meaning of these words in the context of the specific topic, but these words are not high frequency or versatile enough to be taught in our precious 190 opportunities to teach new words.

## THE 80 PER CENT RULE

We now have a greater understanding of the issues surrounding vocabulary and also an improved subject knowledge of the tiers of vocabulary and how we can use them to choose the right words to teach our pupils. But, in the busy world of primary education, we don't want to get too bogged down with spending excessive amounts of time deciphering if a word is Tier 1, 2 or 3. As long as we are in the right area and ask ourselves the questions below, we are going to be choosing the right sort of words. This will allow us to be more consistent and more effective over the period of the whole academic year, and more realistic about what we need to do and how best to spend our valuable time.

Equipped with our new knowledge and using the tiers of vocabulary as a lens to focus on the right words to teach, we are more likely to choose the right type of word. Ask yourself the following questions:

- Is this word likely to be encountered again?
- Is this word going to link or unlock knowledge across the curriculum and future learning?
- Is this word going to enhance, or be useful within, my pupils' writing?

Answering 'yes' on all three is the perfect situation. This means that this word is likely to be Tier 2 and useful for you to teach and for the children to know. Even answering 'yes' for two out of three questions means this word will still be useful.

## SIMPLE BOOKS, SIMPLY EFFECTIVE!

Even some of the simplest books, from the EYFS upwards, will contain huge amounts of vocabulary that we want children to understand and learn, as they will encounter it again and again. So don't discard early story books as they still contain complex and beautiful vocabulary that we want our pupils to learn. They may not be able to read this vocabulary yet independently, but those words can still become part of their spoken and written vocabulary.

For example, *We're Going on a Bear Hunt* by Michael Rosen is short and repetitive but uses some fantastic words that even Year 6 teachers would love to see in their children's writing. Two such words are 'gloomy' and 'narrow'.

**'Gloomy'** is a very high-frequency adjective that will be encountered again and again and will certainly enhance a pupil's writing. So, two out of three. Great.

**'Narrow'** is very high frequency, is very cross-curricular and will link knowledge across a curriculum, and will be useful as part of children's writing! Three out of three! Perfect.

Let's jump to Year 6 where 'gloomy' is used within the first page of *Room 13* by Robert Swindells – a gothic thriller. We've come a long way from the jolly bear hunt but this word is crucial for the experience of the reader and the voice of the writer. This could have been learned in the EYFS or Year 1.

Again in Year 6, a more concrete Tier 2 example is when 'narrow' cropped up in the KS2 maths reasoning paper as part of a three-mark question on area and perimeter. The question was nationally answered poorly because high numbers of pupils didn't understand the word 'narrower' in a question referring to a rectangle. On a national scale, children's understanding of the word 'narrow' was a huge barrier to them answering a question on area and perimeter which was actually pretty straightforward.

Ultimately, it's all about everyone in school being part of this living consciousness, and awareness of vocabulary and the value it offers to pupils.

# 5 – EARLY VOCABULARY DEVELOPMENT IN THE EYFS

Teaching a Word of the Day is a much more formal process that will happen from Year 1 upwards, whereas with EYFS and nursery, we need to start to think about how we can actively promote language development within our earliest provisions. Logically, if we jump back to the research of Hart and Risley (2003), the adult, the conversation and the environment are hugely significant in the development of 86 to 98 per cent of children's vocabularies. Within our EYFS provisions, we therefore need to review how each learning environment promotes positive interactions between adults and children.

## LABELLING

Let's look at the role of labelling in school. The clear intention with labelling objects within EYFS provisions is to promote children's vocabularies and to help them to identify what objects are. In some provisions, there are huge amounts of labels, everywhere, which can often take a considerable amount of time and money to make. But is there actually any impact?

Now, somewhat cynically, it could easily be suggested that labels are highly ineffective because the children in those environments can't independently read them. Nearly all the children found in those settings will be about to begin their journey in phonics and so nearly every label in that setting has very little value when it comes to developing a child's vocabulary. Being aware of this isn't a bad thing – it's good! Armed with this subtle awareness, we can step into our EYFS provisions and easily carry out a visual review of the environment and assess the effectiveness of the labels within.

### LABELLING LINKED TO PHONICS

Remember, we are not banning labels; we are building an awareness of how they can be extremely ineffective if just used blindly without clear thought processes. We would still label children's names on pegs and other extremely important objects within the classroom. If you want to add labels within your EYFS provision, think about matching any form of label to your progression through the phases of phonics. This will develop simple Tier 1 vocabulary, support phonics teaching and provide confidence that children may have some ability to read the simple labels.

## ACTIVATE CONVERSATION! ACTIVATE ENVIRONMENTS!

In order to effectively develop children's vocabularies in the early years, we need to have a clear, simple and consistent approach to developing it, that everyone across the school is aware of.

Hart and Risley (2003) give us the solution we require for EYFS. To develop our pupils' vocabularies, we need to activate conversation within the environment and expose children to waves of spoken vocabulary and speech conventions. But, our focus is not on the children, it is on the adults.

For example, looking at the EYFS setting in the photograph below, we can see an exciting provision for the pupils, one they would never find in their own socio-economic home life. The value and opportunity provided here is huge, but could so easily be missed!

**A tuff tray provocation in an early years setting**

What we must realise is that, within this setting, the vocabulary that has been placed here is not for the pupils but for the adults! Remember, if we agree that the children who come into this environment are unlikely to be able to read these 'labels', then essentially, the labels have no value in their current form. This is because it is the adult, the 'caregiver' of vocabulary language and communication, who is central to any oral or vocabulary development for our children.

This vocabulary has been placed there for the adult. The leader of this environment or classroom teacher has created an amazing tuff tray full of wonderful materials for the children to experience. The vocabulary has been placed there as a prompt for the adults to engage in purposeful conversation and everyone in the EYFS setting must be made aware of their responsibility when they interact with the children.

Every environment that a child could play and learn within should be thoughtfully equipped with essential vocabulary that will enhance and develop their learning. Think carefully though. If we think about the tiers of vocabulary and the example image on page 24, the vocabulary isn't labelling the items (the noun/name). They are in fact looking at the verbs and adjectives associated with the learning opportunity. These will undoubtedly, as the child grows, be encountered in fiction and in real life. These are hugely valuable words that Year 5 and 6 teachers would be delighted to see in a child's writing, that we are starting to embed years before.

The reason why these five, six or seven words are so important is because they provide clarity for everyone on the type of vocabulary that we should be using. Schools often recruit teaching assistants from the school's immediate community (i.e. parents of pupils). If the school is in an area of disadvantage, the TAs' vocabularies may not be wide as you might expect.

We need to be more specific about the type of high-quality conversations that occur in the EYFS. Naturally, adults coming into these environments may chat to pupils about what they might be doing after school or what they had at lunch. Just by providing these few words, each mini environment becomes more highly focused and removes ambiguity. Staff love this. They know the clear expectation and how they can have the biggest impact for the pupils. This is easily done through coaching – skilled staff such as EYFS leads can model conversations and be observed developing conversation skills with pupils.

Whether in the construction area, water table or writing zone, have five, six or seven well-chosen pieces of vocabulary that all adults know they must use within their conversations with children to encourage them to use the words themselves.

And when I say every adult, I mean *every* adult: EYFS leaders, class teachers, cover supervisors, cleaners, site supervisors, teaching assistants, volunteers, supply teachers or head teachers. Everyone who enters these environments with the children becomes a 'caregiver' of language and communication and so has a huge shared responsibility to actively develop the children's vocabularies.

Simple to implement, yet highly effective. Again, this links back to this 'hive mentality' and 'living consciousness' in school that we want to develop, where everyone is aware of their responsibility to the children and the wide impact it can have.

## TO CONVERSATION... AND BEYOND!

Read books aloud! If we think about Hart and Risley (2003) once again, children hearing words, vocabulary and spoken conventions is the key factor in them developing their vocabularies, their subconscious awareness of sentence structure and much more.

Most children will be read aloud to in school, but can we up the ante? Can we do it more regularly, more often each day? It is crucial that we do.

## STORY TIME INTERVENTION

The other element to consider is the social background of your children. There will be children who need stories read to them even more than others, children whose speech, communication skills and vocabularies are underdeveloped. What about introducing a 'story time intervention' for these pupils, which can be delivered by any adult? This would ensure that maybe a specific group of five or six children are targeted and are read short stories and picture books to, four or five times a day. Knowing our pupils and their families can help us make these decisions as to who this type of intervention would be really beneficial for. The best thing is, the children will love it!

Each story might only take five minutes to read to the pupils, but the amount of language they will hear modelled will probably be in excess of anything they have experienced before. This is a really small-time investment for a huge payout; we just need to be consistent.

> **NINJA NOTES**
> We could invest in the story time intervention even more, with a few props, puppets or simple costumes for the children to use and enjoy. So much fun and so powerful!

# 6 – TAUGHT VS ENCOUNTERED VOCABULARY

Believe it or not, discussion around taught vs encountered vocabulary can often turn into heated debate. It's the classic traditional vs progressive teaching debate, or a little bit like the great enduring cream tea debate. Cream tea has been served in the UK since the 11th century and people have ruminated on the order of spreading the scone's traditional toppings ever since. While those in Devon typically spread the clotted cream first followed by the jam, the Cornish tradition is to spread jam first followed by the cream. Decisions, decisions… but, ultimately, who cares? Scones, cream and jam are awesome! All three parts are just as equally important and, quite frankly, delicious. So we can sit around debating which way is better, or we could get stuck in and just eat some scones. I know which I'll be doing *he says while wiping away jammy, creamy crumbs*.

**Next time you have a scone, post a picture! #NinjaScone**

I guess I'm trying to say that the process of eating and enjoying the scones is way more important than debating which type is better, when considering all of the constituent parts are the same. Flipping the context back to vocabulary: if we can appreciate that taught and encountered vocabulary can both offer valuable teaching opportunities, then we are in a much stronger position to increase the word wealth of our pupils.

## TAUGHT VOCABULARY

Let's start to think about what taught vocabulary is and its importance within the classroom. Taught vocabulary encompasses an in-detail, planned approach to vocabulary, where you will 'teach' your pupils about a specific word, all of its associations and all that it encompasses. Planning for the teaching of specific vocabulary is crucial; you can't just rely on high-quality and relevant vocabulary to reveal itself at the moment you require it. Plus, if we rely on chance, we will always be in deficit of our 50,000 words target for our working vocabularies.

We know we only have a short time with our learners over their time in primary education, and even less in secondary, so ensuring we have a clear rationale as to the words we are choosing to expose pupils to is crucial. We can't afford to waste these opportunities. Here are four relevant rationales for teaching vocabulary:

· widening and deepening pupils' vocabulary pools
· targeted teaching of rich vocabulary for writing
· pre-teaching for reading
· general understanding of vocabulary.

### WIDENING AND DEEPENING PUPILS' VOCABULARY POOLS

In the first instance, we may just be aiming to widen a pupil's vocabulary. For example, we might decide to select a word that could act as both a noun and a verb depending on how it is used within a certain sentence. This type of word is extremely useful. It might also be that a word has multiple modifications in terms of prefixes, suffixes, synonyms and antonyms. So by teaching just one word, we are actually exposing a learner to 10–15 other associated words and modifications! The more associations pupils can make with words, the more likely they are to retain this new learning. This is why word choice is so important in the first instance. See the 'Chain' meaning tree, opposite, for an example of what I mean.

Some words may have very few other associations and you might hit a dead end very quickly if you haven't carefully thought about your planned vocabulary opportunities. But, just because a word doesn't have 15+ modifications, doesn't mean it is any less important or valuable in the context you hope it will be used. As a professional, you will need to make this judgement call.

Subject knowledge at this point is a crucial element that will impact on your ability to expertly explain all of the important elements of these specifically chosen words. Do your homework and ensure you understand the morphology of the words you're teaching. For example, you should be up to speed on how tense affects the chosen words and which prefixes can be used with it.

chain (noun)

# 'CHAIN' MEANING TREE

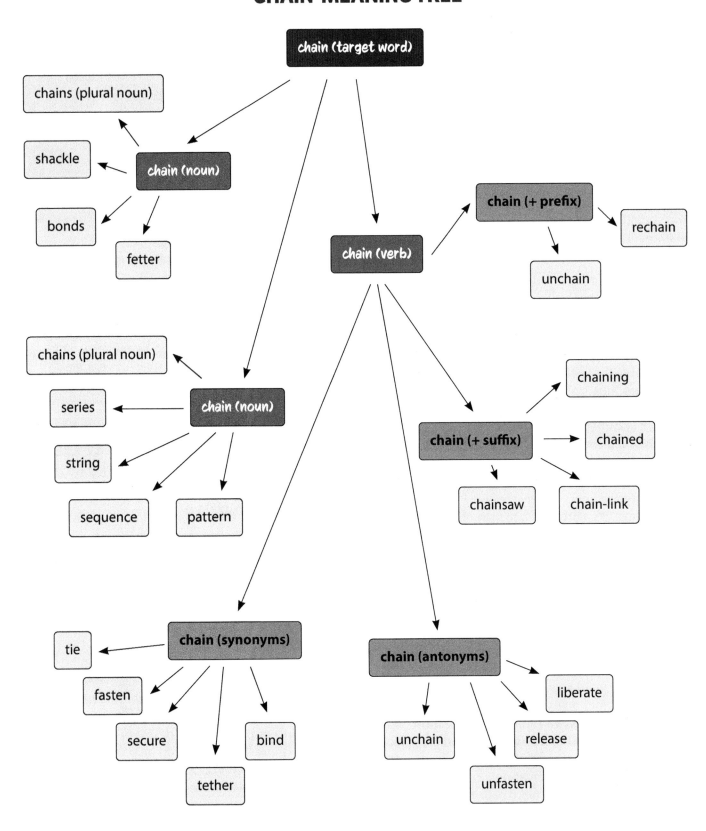

**The meaning tree for the word 'chain'**

**Invest time in yourself. Your own subject knowledge is essential.**

To be confident about teaching a bespoke word each day, a comprehensive subject knowledge and understanding of terminology is essential. Master the basics of your subject knowledge and you will be ready to incorporate taught vocabulary into your teaching practice. The elements suggested below are the most common grammatical areas that will arise when teaching new vocabulary to children. You should be confident in discussing and using them. As suggested earlier, within the taught element of vocabulary, you can plan carefully for the spelling, punctuation and grammar of each word.

You should be confident in discussing and using grammatical terms with your class. At the most basic level, you should understand the following terms and how they apply to any word you are teaching: noun, verb, adjective, determiner, synonym, antonym, suffix, prefix.

## THE WORD PLAN

It's probably the perfect time to discuss Vocabulary Ninja's plans for world domination! Errrm, sorry, that's a different book. I meant plans for word domination. That's right – my word plan. As mentioned earlier, having a sound subject knowledge is crucial in allowing you to flow with discussions and teaching that encountering vocabulary will undoubtedly present. In the first instance, it's a great idea to plan out your knowledge of a word. The word plan isn't necessarily a lesson plan; it's designed to arrange your subject knowledge of the word, ready to discuss with pupils.

Let's make it clear from the outset: Vocabulary Ninja is fully aware of the demands on a modern teacher's time (believe me, I know!). I'm not for one minute advocating that you need to plan for every word that you intend to teach, but it might be useful to organise your word knowledge and child-friendly definitions. Sometimes using a 'new' word in a child-friendly manner can stump even the most knowledgeable teacher but with the word plan, five minutes and a prudent scribble here and there, you're done. You will become increasingly confident with common vocabulary. The word plan will then evolve as a practical tool. It can be used to explore more challenging vocabulary before it is exposed to pupils, ensuring synonyms are relevant, or you could have an example prepared within a multi-clause sentence so that you incorporate SPaG elements into your teaching. Remember: if the objective is to widen pupils' vocabulary, then we must choose words that are going to serve that purpose and meet that objective. Spending 15 minutes on the word 'caravan', a noun, won't offer up much other vocabulary. As a noun, it is what it is – a caravan.

On the next page is an example of how you might complete the word plan document to organise your word knowledge.

**Photocopy, then laminate the blank word plan to use it again. Help the environment and your workload.**

## TARGETED TEACHING OF MEANING-RICH VOCABULARY FOR WRITING

Widening and deepening a pupil's vocabulary has to be an ongoing and conscious part of your daily teaching – adding to your pupil's pool each and every day. The widening of their vocabulary is a very broad objective, a splattering of vocabulary if you will. Much like launching a rock that you can barely carry into a pond, it's going to make a big splash. Everyone and everything in its vicinity are going to get wet, to a greater or lesser degree. Sometimes, though, we might need to be a little more precise with the outcomes we hope to achieve. So, as opposed to widening general vocabulary (which must of course remain a focus), we need depth. In other words, we need to teach a specific word for its rich nature and target its use within writing.

As a professional educator (although I'm not sure there's such a thing as an amateur educator), we can safely assume that you will have a wider and deeper social, academic and literary vocabulary to draw upon than your pupils. Using this vast knowledge of language, and incorporating some of the wonderful resources available to you on the internet and in books, you can teach some very specific meaning-rich words to your pupils. These targeted, meaning-rich words will be chosen by you in the knowledge that they can be used in the very near future, that day even, in a pupil's writing. These words will often be extremely powerful and help the author (your pupil) to elicit emotion from the audience as they read. They are those words that help an author *show* what is happening in their work, rather than simply *telling* the reader.

**Contextualised examples** – Context is crucial for vocabulary learning. Depending on the context that you are talking or writing about, certain associations and modifications will be more or less appropriate for use. From the 'chain' example, one word that hasn't been noted as a synonym is 'moor'. Moor wasn't included in the list of synonyms due to its specific relevance to the context of the ocean and harbours, i.e. 'the boat was moored'. We wouldn't want to use 'moor' as a straight swap for the verb 'chain' in most contexts. Context is crucial.

# WORD PLAN

Vocabulary Ninja © Andrew Jennings, 2019

| Target word: | chain | Text reference: | | *A Christmas Carol*, page 23 |
|---|---|---|---|---|
| Word class: | verb, noun | Pronunciation: | | *chain* |
| Definition: | Noun: A chain is a series of metal hoops that are linked together.<br>Verb: To chain means to attach one thing to another. | | | |
| Contextualised examples: | Noun example: Vocabulary Ninja always ensured he used **a chain** to secure his bicycle.<br>Verb example: It is essential **to chain** your bike to a fence before going inside a shop. | | | |

| Synonyms: | Antonyms: | Prefixes: | Suffixes: | Rhyming words: |
|---|---|---|---|---|
| Noun: bonds, shackles<br>Verb: tie, fasten, secure, tether, bind | Verb: unchain, unfasten, release, liberate | unchain, rechain, interchain | chained, chaining | pain, plain, brain, plane, rain, stain, grain |

24

**Synonyms and antonyms** – These are associations of the word. When I refer to associations, I am typically referring to synonyms and antonyms, as well as variations to nouns. They are words that might be directly or maybe even tenuously linked to the target word. In the 'chain' example, there are 16 words that we might consider as having association (not all of them are included here).

**Prefixes and suffixes** – These are modifications. Generally, the root of the word remains constant with various prefixes and suffixes being added to modify the word and its meaning. Within the 'chain' example there are five examples of modifications. Yet again, the list of modifications provided isn't exhaustive and some more obscure modifications are possible to find.

# WORD PLAN

| Target word: | | |
| --- | --- | --- |
| Word class: | | Text reference: |
| Definition: | | Pronunciation: |
| Contextualised examples: | | |

| Synonyms: | Antonyms: | Prefixes: | Suffixes: | Rhyming words: |
| --- | --- | --- | --- | --- |
| | | | | |

These meaning-rich words will most likely have very few prefixes or suffixes and, in most instances, have no 'context appropriate' synonyms or antonyms – very low association and modification value. Such words don't widen a pupil's general vocabulary, but remember: that's not what we are aiming to achieve by teaching these words. By teaching meaning-rich words, we will add *depth* to our word pool. Power now comes from precision, not the splattering as before. This time, the rock you have chosen has a precise shape, an evenly distributed weight and a smooth texture, perfect for the job you have chosen it for – skimming. When you choose the perfect stone for skimming, the onlookers are entranced as your stone bounces elegantly time after time across the still surface of the water; the same applies to word choice. Enabling pupils to make meaningful and evocative word choices can have a profound effect on the audience. First, we need to facilitate the deepening of word knowledge for pupils to draw upon with independence and purpose.

> **Put an A4 piece of paper with 'prefix' written on it to the left of your whiteboard and an A4 piece of paper with 'suffix' to the right. Refer to these when you're teaching a new word.**

There isn't any significant difference to the manner in which we would approach a meaning-rich word compared to a more common word. The word plan will still be a useful document for organising your ideas, and relevant contextual examples will be so important in ensuring that the children understand the word. In a lot of instances, meaning-rich words will take the form of an adjective or a verb, so having some pertinent images to support your contextual example will help bring the word to life for your learners. Crucially, during this discrete teaching time, giving pupils the opportunity to use the word within a written sentence of their own is essential. This helps embed the word within their own chosen context and also gives less confident writers a practical example of their own to draw upon at a later date. I will refer to this whole teaching process in detail in subsequent chapters.

One of the greatest things about meaning-rich words is that 'real' authors also use them in the children's literature that they write. Pupils who read independently will encounter them on a page-by-page basis, which is fabulous. However, for younger pupils, the less confident and the reluctant readers in your class, you will need to be the fountain from which those words flow through the books you expose them to. For children, giving them the power to use something that an actual author uses in their book is immeasurably valuable. Why? Because children mimic everything that they are exposed to – monkey see, monkey do. Why wouldn't the same be true for vocabulary? The more often learners are exposed to high-quality language, and the more often they are given the opportunity to use it, the more likely it is that this language will become part of the person that they are.

## A LITERAL LITERARY BARRIER

Meaning-rich vocabulary is extremely pupil-specific. We must always remember that 'one child's "huge" is another child's "voracious"'. Here are two case studies of pupils who held words in two very different levels of esteem.

> **'Huge'**
>
> I always remember a specific pupil, and he was representative of 'that type' of pupil. Let's call him Declan. It's easy to look back fondly at that little rascal, but did he make me earn my crust! Wow – it was a slog! A talented footballer and popular in school with his peers, but working way below age-related expectations. In the day to day, it was easy to get bogged down, and to a certain extent, there was most likely little more that could have been done for that pupil in Year 5. He was totally turned off to learning, unwilling to even just try. His behaviour was a product of the barriers he encountered in every moment of the day, especially within academia – a literal literary barrier, constructed from living in a word-impoverished environment. Declan misbehaved because he didn't understand enough words (blunt, right?). For this type of pupil, vocabulary and the associated understanding were crucial to be able to function socially, communicate and engage in learning at a fundamental level. Being able to do this would have been a 'huge' success. In the short time Declan was my pupil, by introducing new vocabulary (along with intensive phonics teaching), he began to exert a level of control and enjoyment in knowing and using his new-found vocabulary-based independence.

> **Find opportunities wherever possible to share fabulous examples of word choices.**

**Sample writing of a voracious pupil**

### 'Voracious'

The true value of teaching vocabulary discretely came to fruition for me via this pupil and her close peer group. Let's call her Meg. She was an avid reader, a talented writer and extremely hard-working. Her writing was good; she knew all of the checklist features, the grammar, the expanded noun phrases, and so on. She could do it all. Teaching vocabulary to Meg was about that next bit – the creation of tension and atmosphere with vocabulary (the bit that's hard to teach). The bit that is easier for children who read, because they're immersed in it all the time. 'Translucent' was the word that had been discretely taught in an earlier lesson, with the knowledge that a dragon would soon be encountered by Sir Lancelot in the text we were reading. We targeted words, such as 'emaciated' too, ready for a piece of writing that was planned for the end of the week. Meg smashed it. Not in the checklist or interim assessment framework sense, but in a sense that mattered to me as I read it. I was proud of her. Her word pool was widening and deepening each day because of her 'voracious' appetite for words, and the impact was clear for all to see. You can see what she wrote above.

For those two very different pupils, words were valuable in two very contrasting ways. For one pupil, words had the potential to open the door to a world of understanding but that door was stubbornly closed. For the other, words enabled the pupil to walk through the door and become immersed in everything held within. In neither scenario were words any more important or valuable than in the other. In both situations, vocabulary had the power to disable or enable them as learners.

Whether in EYFS, Year 6 or Year 10, the language we choose to teach pupils is of the upmost importance. It's continuous, it builds, it widens and it deepens word by word.

## PRE-TEACHING VOCABULARY FOR READING

The pre-teaching of vocabulary is another proactive strategy to use within your taught vocabulary arsenal. As mentioned previously, we don't want to hold either taught or encountered vocabulary in any greater esteem than the other. So let's clarify, so as not to confuse. Pre-teaching doesn't mean we are going to laboriously go through a bank of words and explain them all at the beginning of a book. If anything, it's more about a state of preparedness in yourself. You could even say that the 'pre' in 'pre-teaching' means you as the teacher being prepared so that you can unleash the words at the right moment.

Teach your pupils about words that hold a richness in the context they have been used, but also be aware of words that have the potential to create a barrier to understanding. Think about pupils like Declan and Meg, or even yourself – you don't want to be caught out by a menacingly roguish word, used sublimely by an author, that has you totally foxed. And, although for most teachers this is a very unlikely situation, just think about how much more likely this is to happen to your pupils and what they will feel if it happens too often. By having a greater state of preparedness, we are increasing our learners' capacity to access, understand and engage with the text.

The online education community is a fabulous place to gather and magpie ideas for your own teaching practice. Within this community, vocabulary, the role it plays within the classroom and the pedagogy that underpins it is growing in prominence. It's wonderful to see how teachers of all experience levels are honing in on the value that vocabulary can add.

*NINJA REFLECTIONS*

Yet again time becomes a factor. 'When am I supposed to fit this all in?' I hear you cry. But, being prepared for the vocabulary that is used within a text will enable you to spend your valuable time in school to far greater effect. I suggest you super-charge your vocabulary book. Make it a hugely valuable resource to work from. Highlight, make notes, underline, annotate key vocabulary in the book you're reading. Once you have done it once, you won't need to do it again and chances are you'll use it time and time again! And remember, not every word will need discussing, but surely it's better to be prepared for the ones that do.

Vocabulary Ninja © Andrew Jennings, 2024

## GENERAL UNDERSTANDING OF VOCABULARY

The final rationale for teaching vocabulary for general understanding can be made very simple: there are words that you will inevitably and innocently assume that your pupils know but, believe me, they don't. One of my greatest oversights as a class teacher, and this remains true today, is assuming that a pupil knows what a word means.

Words that you wouldn't especially choose for their depth, their capacity to expand vocabulary or their effect on the atmosphere in a text – I mean 'general' words that you and many other adults will use in normal everyday activities – they can just wash over your pupils because they don't know what they mean! Here are two very recent examples, both with Year 6 pupils, believe it or not, who both went on to achieve the all-important expected standard in consecutive years.

### 'Fortnight'

Amidst a conversation linked to half-term, I dared to ask the question, 'Do we all know what a fortnight is?'. I don't even recall why. Uneasy expressions and awkward body language followed. It wasn't just one pupil who didn't know the meaning of the word, although she became the focus of the discussion. It wasn't her fault; she just didn't know what it meant. Now she does, they all do, which is great.

### 'Countryside'

In a very recent lesson observation, I was keen to impress and had gone all out, only for the lesson to be stopped in its tracks by several pupils who had no idea what 'the countryside' was. Something so very simple that I just assumed all pupils would know. They didn't, but they do now.

The key message here is that every child's vocabulary will vary because of the different environments they experience. We must never assume that a child knows what a word means; we must be vigilant, be ninja and ready to pounce on every opportunity to teach new vocabulary to our pupils and increase their understanding. We can't plan for these words – it's impossible – but because of their 'general' and 'everyday' nature, we can be ready to challenge pupil understanding and ready to seize on every opportunity to increase word wealth.

# ENCOUNTERED VOCABULARY

There shouldn't really be a debate about taught (contextless) vs encountered (contextual) vocabulary. Hopefully, you have already begun to understand how they shouldn't be seen as mutually exclusive, but are essential to each other's survival. One can't really be seen to function effectively without the other. If we are to become ninja in the classroom, then every new piece of vocabulary is important, regardless of whether it is taught or encountered.

Encountered vocabulary is quite simply the vocabulary found in a book – the specific, articulate and purposeful word choices that an author makes. It's certainly easy to see why this drum is firmly banged by a whole host of educators and professionals. 'It must be taught in context!' they cry. 'The contexts, atmospheres, emotions, characters and plots give the words a purpose and bring them to life.' This is certainly true. But encountered vocabulary is only valuable to our pupils if *we* have the ninja mentality – that state of preparedness, ready to pounce. Not every teacher in the kingdom is a master of the written word (nor am I). We have to work at it every day, to be ready to bring the words to life as we encounter them. The words need to encounter you – you're not to be messed with! You mean business.

Encountered vocabulary, executed with skill, is underpinned by the principals of taught vocabulary – pre-reading and ensuring the vocabulary is ready to encounter you. This mentality is crucial. 'Encountering' something implies that it is an unexpected incident, but we don't really want this to be a recurring pattern. If we encountered wild animals while out walking in the forest each day and didn't modify our behaviour patterns, eventually our luck would run out and we might 'encounter' a bear. Not cool – the consequences would most likely be catastrophic. If we aren't ready to encounter a particular word, then the consequences for our pupils can be just as catastrophic. It may sound a little dramatic, but even the increased contextual value of encountered vocabulary alone won't save you. What you need is an encountered vocabulary mindset.

## ENCOUNTERED VOCABULARY MINDSET

Mindset is of paramount importance if you are to become a Vocabulary Ninja. Your thought processes inevitably determine your actions, and your actions will determine any outcomes you hope to achieve. Your mindset is everything. A ninja can be defined as a person who excels in a particular skill. In order to excel and start master vocabulary, you must first master your ninja mindset.

When it comes to encountered vocabulary, we need to be fully prepared. Vocabulary needs to encounter you! Adapting the strategies opposite will ensure that you make the most of every vocabulary-based encounter that comes your way.

**Trim or cut a school book in half or create a folded booklet. Use it as a mini word recorder – The Word Explorer's Journal!**

NINJA NOTES

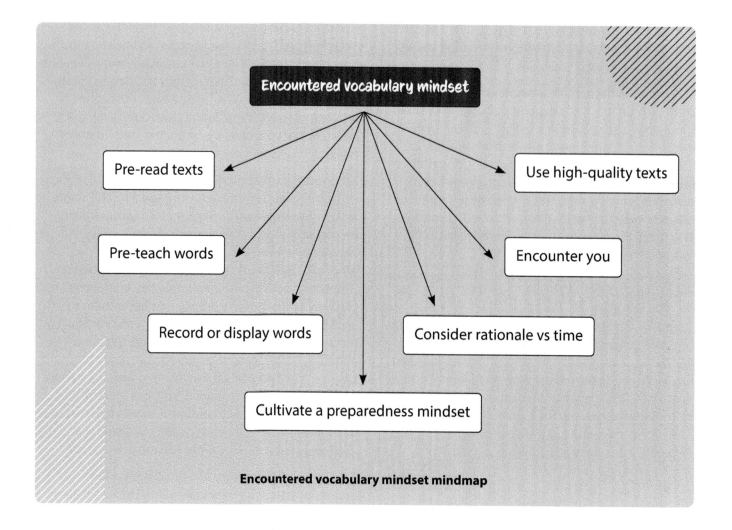

**Encountered vocabulary mindset mindmap**

## How to 'encounter' vocabulary

**Pre-read texts** – Pre-read the books that you intend to share with your learners. Highlight, mark and make notes in the text. Be knowledgeable about the literature.

**Pre-teach words** – Be realistic – you might choose to teach one word from each chapter in greater detail. These words will undoubtedly appear in other texts. These will be uncovered during your pre-read and then planned for.

**Record or display words** – Any words that you take the time to speak about, knowledge-check or teach in greater detail should be recorded somewhere in the classroom for pupils to reference. You could use a working wall, vocabulary books or display. This is crucial if you are to develop independent learners. (See Chapter 5.)

**Cultivate a preparedness mindset** – As an adult, you will pre-read a book and make assumptions about the language that is important for your pupils to know; this will also be informed by the words that you know. Be prepared for your best-laid plans to be foiled by simple words that your pupils don't understand. Still teach your meaning-rich language, but be prepared for the everyday language barriers that will arise from the text. These words will often need a very brief explanation and then you can simply move on. There isn't time for anything more.

**Consider rationale vs time** – Not every word can be dissected to a morphological level; let's be real – schools are hectic places to be. A single book will hold thousands of words. What is your rationale for teaching a word? Is it for understanding, for use in writing or to widen vocabulary? Be clear on what you hope to achieve by teaching a word. Think about which words only need a quick understanding check or a ten-second explanation and move on. Also think about those meaning-rich words that you want pupils to devour and replicate in their writing – these words might need recording for later.

**Encounter you** – Just think about being unprepared for an encounter with a wild animal such as a wolf or a bear. The outcome isn't going to be pleasant. It's much better to be ready for those encounters, and it's the same with vocabulary.

**Use high-quality texts** – Use high-quality texts with your class. Social media is a wonderful resource to find high-quality texts, from classical authors to ones bursting onto the literary scene!

Remember, there will never be enough time to teach every word. It's impossible. Believe in the value of the words that you have chosen and know that there really is only so much that you can do. Each micro-success and the marginal gains that you make will be of significance in the end.

> **NINJA REFLECTIONS**
>
> Huge or voracious, Cornwall or Devon, taught vs encountered – all equally important, equally valuable and equally tasty! There isn't the need to debate which is better; we need them all. By focusing on that very fact, we can begin to think about the explicit instruction of vocabulary and how to make it memorable.

# 7– EXPLICIT VOCABULARY INSTRUCTION

This part of the book is where we start to think about explicit vocabulary instruction on a daily basis. Even at this early stage, understanding that explicit vocabulary instruction will make up only a small part of your assault on vocabulary is important; it isn't the only tool you will be using.

If you were to think about our magical target of 50,000 words in a child's working vocabulary, teaching a word a day for seven years would still only equate to 1,330 words for pupils with 100 per cent attendance. This is why explicit vocabulary instruction alone mustn't be your only focus. It must be one of many effective strategies in your vocabulary toolkit which are ready to be used when the opportunity presents itself.

Not every word can be planned for, nor should it be, and so a range of other effective strategies outlined in later chapters should be used in conjunction with explicit vocabulary instruction as part of your teaching repertoire. This is when we begin to think about taught vs encountered vocabulary.

Explicit instruction is still crucial for a number of reasons. As discussed earlier, the role that grammar now plays within the curriculum is significant. Explicit instruction offers a number of detailed grammatical avenues to explore with your pupils and, more importantly, the time to do it effectively. Due to the nature of encountered vocabulary, it isn't always planned for, and will only enable a short discussion at that point. Exploring the grammar of encountered vocabulary in detail during a fast-paced English or maths lesson probably wouldn't be good practice.

So, what do we mean by explicit vocabulary instruction? Well, by explicit, I mean 'stated clearly and in detail, leaving no room for confusion or doubt'. This is the single most important principle of teaching vocabulary. Such a fabulous definition, a mantra even! Even in this statement, we are simply discussing teaching and learning.

'Explicit means stated clearly and in detail, leaving no room for confusion or doubt.'

*What you do        so that others can learn*

**Teaching        Learning**

Using the strategies and advice that follow, you can attempt to maximise the effectiveness of the 'what you do' part.

## WORD OF THE DAY

Teaching a Word of the Day (WOD) should be a core component of your vocabulary systems in school. The routine alone – explicitly teaching a single word each day – will benefit your pupils. As stated in previous chapters, your rationale for teaching this word will need to be clear in your mind. Alternatively, *Vocabulary Ninja* provides Grasshopper and Shinobi-level words to teach every day of the academic year. Grasshopper level words are aimed at ages 4–7 and Shinobi level words at 7–11-year-old children. The caveat being that we can never pigeonhole a word to a certain age of learner but should teach them what they require.

Have the Word of the Day up when children enter the classroom in the morning. This is purposeful and great for routine.

The principles of teaching a WOD are exactly the same, whether you chose to use a word from *Vocabulary Ninja* or a word of your own. School can be a busy and high-pressure environment, so some days it's good to know that *Vocabulary Ninja* is there – a few clicks and you are ready to go, safe in the knowledge that there will be a high-quality, engaging resource for you to use every day. If you are at the stage of going it alone, *Vocabulary Ninja* provides a range of free resources to teach your own Word of the Day. Simply go to www.vocabularyninja.co.uk.

# TEN STEPS IN TEN MINUTES (ISH!)

Teaching the Word of the Day should be a fast-paced, fun and energetic experience for your learners. The following ten steps are crucial to ensuring it is exactly that. Always keep in mind that this short period of time is your domain – you are teaching and the children are learning. This is the 'what you do' period, where you will work to ensure that there is no confusion or doubt for learners.

**Ninjas don't like sitting at their desks, so get up, move around and create an excitement about the session.**

## Step 1 – Introduce pronunciation (30 seconds)

Introduce the Word of the Day (WOD) to your learners. (See page 55.) The first step is to orally model the WOD: pronounce it clearly, ensuring pupils hear it. Ask the pupils to say the WOD back to you as a group, or perhaps even individually. This may be especially important in regions where certain sound patterns may be affected by dialect or with pupils who you want to ensure are pronouncing the word accurately.

## Step 2 – Clap syllables (30 seconds)

This may be incorporated into Step 1. Reference the syllables of the word. Model clapping the syllables, and get the children to repeat them. Don't ask for conjecture from learners about how many syllables a WOD has – just teach it. You could adapt claps into ninja hand chops and kicks, bringing in a kinaesthetic element to the teaching.

## Step 3 – Explicit definition (60 seconds)

We don't want any confusion about the word; be explicit to ensure there is no doubt about its meaning. Use a child-friendly definition or explain the meaning of the word within the context of the book you are using. Offer additional child-friendly explanation if required. In defining this word, Step 4 should naturally follow when discussing the role the WOD plays within the sentence.

## Step 4 – Discuss word class (30 seconds)

This is where subject knowledge becomes essential. We don't want to be caught offering cliché, simplistic definitions of verbs or adjectives are. The WOD (page 54) will suggest single or multiple word classes that a target word may be able to function as. For instance, a word may be a noun or a verb depending on the role it plays within a sentence, e.g. 'phone' can be a noun (a phone) or a verb (to phone). Discussing the word class within the exemplar sentence can also be extremely useful.

## Step 5 – Display the exemplar sentence (60 seconds)

The exemplar sentence is the first opportunity for learners to see a word in action, allowing for the definition and word class to develop a context in which to be discussed further. Yet again, the exemplar sentence should be as child-friendly as possible to aid understanding. Even at this early stage, some learners will have a greater understanding of a word than others, so a child-friendly example that they can use is essential. You may even offer up another sentence orally that can provide further clarity. Try to ensure that all other words in your examples are familiar – we want the only new word to be the WOD.

## Step 6 – Oral creation and rehearsal (30 seconds)

Ask learners to orally create their own sentence that includes the WOD and share it with the children next to them or on their table. This will allow pupils to hear ideas and contexts from other pupils, as well as drawing inspiration from the exemplar sentence. Adaptation of the word tense is fine, as some children will naturally develop a sentence in the past tense linked to their own memories. Some children will also, without consciously thinking about it, add prefixes and suffixes to the target word. This can be encouraged and celebrated when sharing; definitely make reference to this and the related grammatical terminology if it happens. The oral creation stage is an important opportunity for you to target specific learners and help develop their ideas. Remember, never assume – earn your pennies, circulate around your learners and impact understanding. In other words, teach.

## Step 7 – Orally share (90 seconds)

As we aim to maintain the pace of the session, don't wait for every child to have 'finished' and have a perfect oral sentence to share. Some learners will naturally be ready to share much more quickly. By now, learners will have heard your sentence and three or four examples from the children on their table. Hush the class and ask the children who are ready to start to share their sentence with the class (one at a time). This will ensure that children whose ideas don't come as easily are exposed to further examples of the target word in action and can draw inspiration for themselves. For those children who do have high-quality ideas, refer them to Steps 8 and 9 once Step 7 is complete.

## Step 8 – Orally edit and challenge (60 seconds)

As pupils orally share their sentence with the rest of the class, this is your opportunity to edit the sentences that the pupils have created. This is an extremely powerful tool. We don't want to pick apart every word but selecting a word to improve, correcting the tense or even ensuring subject–verb agreement is in place can be done efficiently at this moment. The great thing about orally editing as you go with pupils is that you can ensure that you are having an instant impact on their understanding. More often than not, the oral feedback you offer to one pupil is pertinent to a group of pupils or even the whole class. Once pupils have shared an idea and you are confident they have grasped the target word, move them quickly on to Step 9. Continue to move quickly through the class, listening to and orally editing as many sentences as possible. Steps 7, 8 and 9 could be streamlined further by having any additional adults work specifically with groups of pupils to ensure the process is expedited. Some children won't need any level of oral editing.

## Step 9 – Write (180 seconds)

Once orally edited, children should record the sentence they have created. Try to do this in the same place to build a working resource bank of vocabulary for pupils to reference independently. This could be in the back of an English book or a specific vocabulary book.

## Step 10 – Share, orally edit and celebrate (60 seconds)

It is crucial to share the written version of the sentence. Pupils will often edit or correct themselves having had the opportunity to read the sentence aloud. If they don't, this is your chance to orally edit the sentence and give some extremely powerful feedback to pupils. Ensure that they immediately act upon that feedback and physically edit their written sentence. At this point, it is also great to remember that one child's 'huge' will be another child's 'voracious'. Celebrate all sentences equally! After you've completed the ten steps, ensure that the WOD is added to your working vocabulary display (see Chapter 8). Having taught the word, you want it to be available for pupils to use and spell independently.

## INSTANTANEOUS SUPERFICIAL IMPACT

Most certainly, teaching the Word of the Day will take a little longer than ten to 15 minutes in the first instance. Your confidence will grow day by day and the pupils will become accustomed to the conventions and WOD routine, which will speed up certain aspects of the session. For instance, some pupils will become extremely eager to produce their written sentence as they already have an exciting idea. Don't get in their way – let them go with it and use Step 7 and beyond. Undoubtedly, there will be days where the Word of the Day is easier to process or understand for pupils and other days where words are a little more tricky. An example might be the word 'fastidious', which can't just be shoehorned into a sentence because it requires contextual and conventional understanding from the pupils. In the case of 'fastidious', a little more work will be required to ensure all pupils can access the WOD.

**Chill! Don't worry if you have to miss sections out. Sometimes classrooms are busy and things crop up.**

One of the subtle brilliances of Word of the Day is that it has an instantaneous superficial impact and a more meaningful, deeper impact too, much like an asteroid striking the Earth. Smaller asteroids or meteorites strike the Earth every day. They don't change the Earth one by one, but they are noticeable. Over time, small interstellar objects striking the surface of the Earth will change, sculpt and modify its entire complexion, maybe until it is entirely unrecognisable. Word of the Day is the same – you will quickly see the WOD cropping up in conversation, and in reading and writing. It's amazing to see! But your daily barrage of discussion, oral editing and challenge, sharing, written opportunities and playfulness with the WOD will have a deeper and more meaningful impact on your pupils. The bonus being that Word of the Day won't rain down terror and destroy the Earth in a strike!

Be aware that understanding will take time. Yes, we will have that instantaneous superficial impact noticeable in conversation and the pupils' books, which as teachers we all want, but don't get too carried away. Remember that it is the cumulative effect over time – the marginal gains, consistency and quality of your subject knowledge – that will build understanding.

For the ultimate impact, try to embed the Word of the Day practice in every class across the school. This won't happen overnight, but just imagine the ninja mindset flowing through your school like a river, filling up your pupils' vocabulary puddles and turning them into vast reservoirs! Once it does happen, a cataclysmic change will happen in your school. It will be like the school has actually been hit by a vocabulary asteroid – an extinction-level event and the dawning of a new era. But before all of that can happen, the first meteor has to strike.

# 8 – THE VOCABULARY ENVIRONMENT – YOUR CLASSROOM

Your classroom has the potential to be the biggest and most effective resource in your vocabulary arsenal. Your classroom environment and the routines found within your classroom are crucial in supporting your vocabulary journey and in further developing the independence of your learners. Having effective systems for recording, displaying and referencing vocabulary will enhance all areas of your curriculum and bring writing and oracy to the forefront of you and your learners' attention. Implementing high-quality working walls can prove hugely beneficial. Throwing out the doubled- or triple-backed dormant display rule book and embracing a 'live' display attitude is invaluable. Children will begin to understand that the walls are full of language that has been taught, discussed and previously used; they will understand what it means and be ready to use it.

The only principle that we need to consider while thinking about our environment is that of effectiveness. Ask yourself the question when looking at a display, 'How effective is this display or use of space?' When I say effective, what I really mean is, how does what you have put on the wall help expedite the learning process in your classroom? How does it respond and adapt to your pupils' needs and the progress that they are making day by day? How does it allow them to continue working independently without your support? If it doesn't, then why not?

Does your display look nice? Is it bright and colourful? Is it double-backed? Is it laminated? Does it remain there for a significant period of time without any aspects changing? These are all superficial aspects that ultimately add no real determinable value to the learning process. And, they take up a huge amount of someone's time to put up there. I know there will be thousands of very similar displays all around the country (and possibly the world) that are from resource suppliers, and look amazing when you walk into a classroom, but how effective are they really? How often are they referred to in your teaching and learning time? How often do pupils use them independently or refer to them in conversations? I wouldn't hesitate to guess that the answer is 'not often'!

By the way, if this is your classroom right now, this isn't a criticism – no chance. It's a reflection point about how, as ninja practitioners, we can draw upon and improve an aspect of our practice to create yet another marginal gain. Your displays won't revolutionise your outcomes, but what they have the potential to do is enhance your practice by that one per cent. As we have already discussed, one per cent on its own isn't worth writing home about, but the accumulation of marginal gains you have already made are definitely worth significant attention. All of these marginal gains may add up to a ten or 15 per cent change over time. Now who would say no to that?

**Correct yourself in front of pupils and staff. Model the thinking behind your word choices.**

## LIVE, RESPONSIVE AND IMMERSIVE ENVIRONMENT

Let's begin to think about effective strategies for recording, displaying and referencing vocabulary in your classroom as aspects that are worth investing your time in. By developing simple routines and investing a small amount of preparation time into your resources, you will quickly supercharge your classroom environment and make it a live, responsive and immersive environment where pupil independence is high and outcomes across the curriculum are improved.

The vocabulary display strategies model I will explain here shows the journey that a piece of vocabulary takes from source through to independent use by pupils and learners within the enabled environment. The model demonstrates how a vocabulary-enabled environment can contribute to increased independence over time and thus improve outcomes.

# VOCABULARY DISPLAY STRATEGIES MODEL (2018)

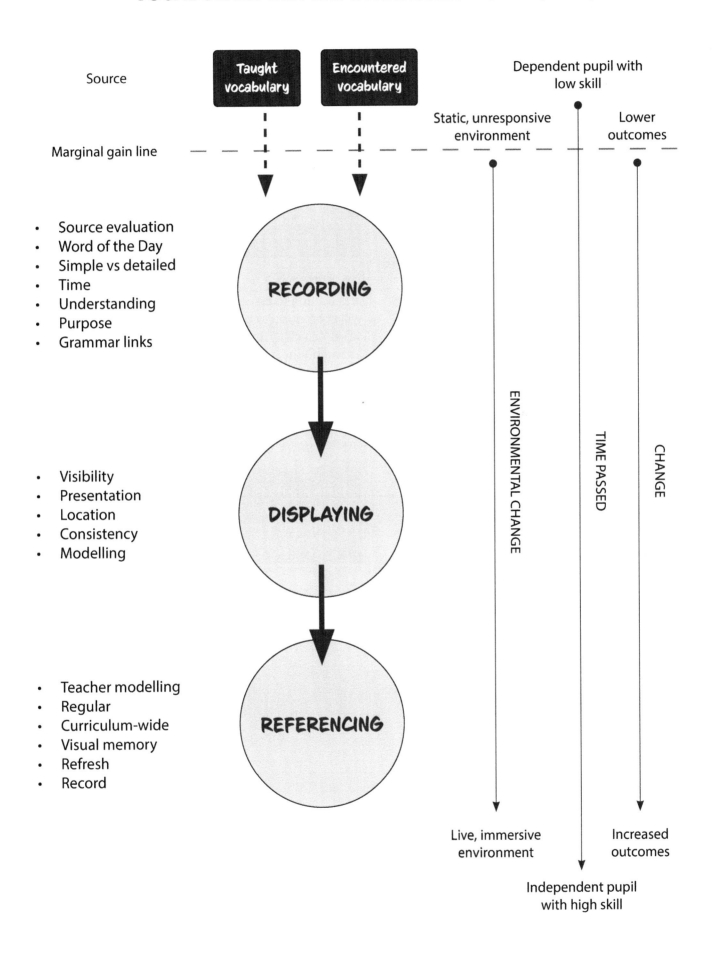

Source

**Taught vocabulary**

**Encountered vocabulary**

Dependent pupil with low skill

Marginal gain line

Static, unresponsive environment

Lower outcomes

- Source evaluation
- Word of the Day
- Simple vs detailed
- Time
- Understanding
- Purpose
- Grammar links

**RECORDING**

- Visibility
- Presentation
- Location
- Consistency
- Modelling

**DISPLAYING**

ENVIRONMENTAL CHANGE

TIME PASSED

CHANGE

- Teacher modelling
- Regular
- Curriculum-wide
- Visual memory
- Refresh
- Record

**REFERENCING**

Live, immersive environment

Increased outcomes

Independent pupil with high skill

## The source

Before we start to think about how we will record vocabulary, it is crucial to think about the source of our vocabulary. The source of vocabulary will directly affect how we respond and what actions we take. Vocabulary will either be taught, e.g. Word of the Day, or it will be encountered incidentally, e.g. in books, conversations and other stimuli that we hadn't necessarily planned on teaching. Even though we had not planned on teaching this language, as a Vocabulary Ninja, we need to be ready to pounce on these opportunities when they arise.

## The marginal gain line

One of the most interesting factors within the model is the 'marginal gain line', which links to overall classroom display effectiveness. Thinking again about the world of sport, the gain line is the line showing the positive progress you have made on the playing field with respect to where you first started. We can take this principle and adapt it to vocabulary display within the classroom and the marginal gains we hope to make by adapting our display practice. The model suggests that unless vocabulary reaches the recording, displaying and referencing stages, we cannot make positive progress beyond the marginal gain line. In essence, a huge of amount of vocabulary is lost because in the first instance it isn't recorded and/or displayed. In the end, it becomes nearly impossible to refer back to it effectively or for all pupils to use it with independence and skill. Just imagine how much vocabulary is lost or how many times our pupils miss the opportunity to embed a word into their working vocabulary. In order for pupils to start making the improvements we so desire, vocabulary has to cross the 'marginal gain line' and progress through the subsequent stages.

These are the three clear stages in the vocabulary display strategies model: recording, displaying and referencing vocabulary. These three stages all occur after vocabulary has been taught or encountered. Within the three core stages of effective vocabulary display strategies, there are also sub-categories that should be considered at each stage. Some of these considerations can be built into an efficient recording, displaying and referencing routine within the classroom.

## Preparation

Like any journey, we must be prepared and well resourced if we are to reach the promised land. Most school supply cupboards and teacher stationery drawers will contain all of the basic supplies that you will require.

## Vocabulary display essentials:

- A4 and A3 card of various colours, trimmed into different lengths, shapes and sizes
- Marker pens of various colours
- Metre stick (or large ruler)
- Sticky tack
- Drawing pins
- Pegs
- String
- Flip chart paper

**Ensure all adults in your classroom understand the new resources and routines. This can help increase their effectiveness and impact.**

Have all of these resources readily available, pre-cut and waiting to be accessed at a moment's notice. This will enable you to build the immersive and responsive, word-rich classroom that you are aiming for. The added bonus is that your pupils will love it even more if they are involved in the process of building and adding to it. Nothing here is a huge revelation – anyone can implement this simple and effective preparation in 15–20 minutes and then be well stocked up for a unit of work and beyond.

**Having these resources hanging in folders or units from the display will make it simpler to add vocabulary as it arises.**

**WOD slips in the classroom**

A little bravery is required here. That pristine, laminated display is great, and I'm sure that the 25–30 hours' work that went into creating it was worthwhile but now I want you to tear it down, leaving only a blank display board with possibly some awesome lettering. With this, you're ready to go. The vocabulary and phrases will be added slowly, but they will create a meaningful display over time, one that has a clear purpose and a role within your classroom. Your teaching assistant or meaningful others will also thank you for not asking them to spend a huge amount of time and money on printing and laminating generic display paraphernalia (what a word by the way!).

Once you have your essentials assembled, you are ready to begin your display adventure and give your classroom a literary heartbeat.

## Recording

How you record your vocabulary will depend on the source – whether it is taught or encountered. Has it come from the Word of the Day, from your class novel, a conversation or your literacy lesson? This is important to be ready for.

As mentioned in Chapter 7, your Word of the Day instruction is a closed procedure with a very clearly defined process and outcomes. As suggested, it is good practice for pupils to have the opportunity to write experimental sentences as part of the Word of the Day activity. This might be in the back of their literacy books or even in another 'vocabulary book' that you use (teachers usually get rather creative with such things). This is all fabulous to see. However, we must consider how readily available the WODs are, that we have spent so much valuable time teaching. I would advise that your classroom has some direct way of *recording* and *displaying* your WODs, so that they can be referenced independently by your pupils at any time of the day (notice the record, display and reference cycle).

**An example vocabulary display or working wall**

Use the windows! Grab some fluorescent drywipe pens and record WODs on the windows. #MarginalGains

Ensuring that words are recorded and displayed effectively means that pupils can, and will, use them independently across the school day and hopefully beyond. It also means that any word can be referenced at any point of the day. You'll be surprised at the number of opportunities you will find to refer back to the WODs you have displayed. A very simple, yet effective, process.

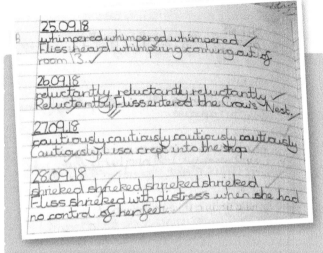

### WOD literacy book

Here is a further example of how the WOD might be progressively recorded in the back of a literacy book. The example shows the learner actively experimenting with the WOD. If the vocabulary book is available in lessons, it serves as a useful reference point for pupils during lessons.

Deciding whether to record a word in a simple or more detailed manner will depend on a range of factors. Time, desired outcome, children's current level of understanding, value, usefulness, possible modifications, and links to spelling, punctuation, grammar and purpose will all affect whether or not you choose to record a word in a simple or detailed fashion. It is prudent to ensure that any detailed recording of vocabulary, which will undoubtedly take up more time, has a clear purpose. These will most likely be words that you purposefully choose to introduce to pupils via the Word of the Day activity, from a class text, and so on. In terms of outcomes, the words you choose to record and display in a more detailed fashion may have been chosen with the knowledge that the words will become essential language for an upcoming piece of writing or drama that the pupils are creating.

You could record the WOD simply (using the working wall), or you could record it in detail. The source is irrelevant really; the key thing here is to ensure that if you and the children are going to spend time recording it in a detailed manner, the outcomes are worth it. In contrast, sometimes it will simply be effective to come across a word, celebrate and explain it, record it (two to three minutes, if that) and move on. Boom – done – slap it up on the word wall! The word has been efficiently recorded, effectively displayed, and now it's available to be referenced readily.

If and when you record a word to be displayed, please write it large enough and clearly enough for every pupil in the room to be able to see it. Too many times, words are recorded (which is amazing), then displayed, but the words are so small that children are required to move much closer, squint even, to see the language. When it comes to recording vocabulary, bigger is better.

**If your writing isn't clear, get a pupil or another adult in the classroom to do it.**

## Displaying

Now you've recorded your vocabulary, in a legible style and in an appropriate font size, you're ready to display your vocabulary.

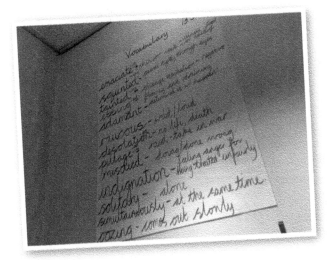

**A classroom where vocabulary is added as part of all aspects of the curriculum.**

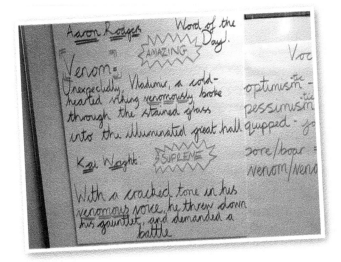

**An example vocabulary display with consistent colours, formats and reference points. Pupils enjoy experimenting with vocabulary and being part of the recording and display process.**

Content that has been taught over a period of several months should be displayed around the classroom on flipchart paper in the form of a poster. Once this information has been on display and referred to regularly, ask pupils to close their eyes and prompt them to point to the posters that you specify. By displaying important taught content around the classroom, and referring to it regularly, you can help create a picture in pupils' heads of where this familiar information prompt is held. One important factor to note is that when the displayed content is referred to, you should adjust your location in the classroom and stand next to the content you are referring to.

Pupils will develop excellent visual retention of the locations of the content. They will be able to discuss what information was in that location and refer to the details. All of the vocabulary and content that you display must be placed intentionally so that it is visible from any seating position in the classroom. Washing lines and pegs can be used to hang language in prominent positions within the classroom. The use of colour is important to stimulate memory and aid recall within the pupils' brains; try to develop a consistent system or pattern when choosing which colour to use. One other area to consider when displaying vocabulary is your modelling and presentation. As a Vocabulary Ninja, you have high standards, you are methodical and are the exemplar that all grasshoppers look towards for guidance.

Vocabulary Ninja © Andrew Jennings, 2024

Before you display anything you have recorded, be sure to think about the location of the vocabulary you wish to present. How visible is it to everyone? Is it large enough to see and is it written clearly enough for all pupils to use independently, without guidance? Does this mean that words need to be printed rather than joined, so that there are no grey areas? Clarity is key. Once you have begun to display vocabulary, how consistently are you recording and displaying the language? Can you create coloured patterns that will aid how effectively your pupils will reference and retain the language? For instance, when you write a verb, can it always be green (or another designated colour)? When you write an adjective, can it always be red? This consistency of colour will aid your pupils' retention. You wouldn't need to do it for every word class – nouns, verbs, adjectives and conjunctions would be fine to begin with.

That's right – there's lots to think about! And you thought displays were straightforward! Well, they are – yours are now going to be just a little bit more ninja.

## Referencing

So, you have recorded lots of awesome vocabulary that you have taught and encountered, you have displayed it effectively so that everyone can see it – you are nearly there and should be commended for your efforts so far. The final stage is referencing the vocabulary that you have recorded and displayed.

Referencing is all about your practice, embedding high-quality language into all aspects of your life within the classroom. Why? Well, if you model it, then the children will begin to replicate your ninja attitude towards words. Emphasise the fact that you are referring back to where the language has been displayed when you use it. Point, gesticulate and orally model your intentions close to the language. The Grand Masters among us will have pre-taught language that will occur in future chapters of class texts or literature you are using, thus creating the awe-inspiring moment when the word we recently taught miraculously turns up in the literature. Perfect!

**Squeeze referenced words into assemblies and model making enhanced vocabulary choices when you make a poor one. #PowerfulStuff**

Find opportunities to use the words that have been displayed in your day-to-day language. If 'tedious' is now on the wall, reference the wall and use the word. Model, explain why you made this language choice, and ask the children why they think you made this choice. What is the effect of using it? This will help knowledge retention and deepen pupils' understanding of the word. If this becomes a staple practice of your classroom, then your pupils will eventually begin to replicate your vocabulary choices and practices.

It was once said that people will only use the vocabulary that their environment demands of them. So the message is clear: I demand that you create an environment that demands more of your pupils. It is your responsibility to create a living, breathing, word-rich environment that demands everything from your grasshoppers, and yourself. You all deserve it. I know that much is true.

**Sometimes space is limited. If you can't have an immersive classroom where vocabulary is dominant on all four walls, at least create a dedicated space for it to be accessible.**

# 9 – IMPROVING WRITING STANDARDS

As teachers, it's essential that we consistently model how to make improving word choices within our writing. We need to grow our pupils' awareness of the positive or negative impact that words can have on the reader.

## WRITING FOR THE READER

Let's consider the role of vocabulary within the sentence; each word conveys meaning for the reader and allows them to understand what the author is trying to say. This happens whether this is across a whole piece of writing or within a single sentence. A great place to start with pupils starting to understand the power of each word is by focusing on just three words. This child-friendly starting point helps to make the impact of improved vocabulary choices become concrete rather than abstract.

### GOT, GET, WENT

The words **'got'**, **'get'** and **'went'** have the power to do both evil and good– they *absolutely* have superpowers when it comes to writing! These three words tend to be commonly overused within children's writing and can negatively impact the meaning and cohesion of individual sentences.

Cohesion within sentences is all about 'flow' and can be quite an abstract concept for pupils to understand. But, other than sentence structure, their vocabulary choices will be the most significant factor that will impact on cohesion. So, we need pupils to have a more concrete understanding of the impact of their word choices on the reader. Let's have a closer look at the problem.

### The problem

The problem with **'got'**, **'get'** and **'went'** happens when they are overused, and children will overuse them when they have limited vocabularies. The problem is that these words tend to offer very little inference. They are 'empty' or 'hollow' verbs. As readers our brains automatically want to imagine, build a picture, make predictions and draw on other knowledge to make links and understand what we are reading. Essentially these sentences become statements and just 'tell' the reader; they state a fact, inhibiting the reader's natural instinct to make inferences.

If we think about sentence structure here, we need a subject and a verb to have a complete sentence. The verb, which will occur in every possible sentence a child might write, is therefore central to the reader's understanding of the text.

And so a pupil's awareness of the verb in all sentences is absolutely paramount to the ongoing development of any child as a writer. Ultimately for teachers and pupils, understanding this helps to take sentence-level cohesion back to the building blocks of the sentence and ensures a more concrete understanding for everyone. It's taking 'show not tell' right back to step one: the individual words.

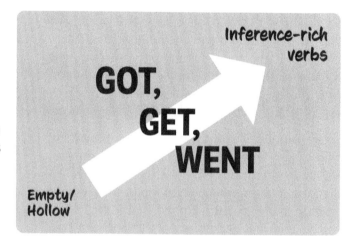

### The solution – one word at a time

As we build a greater awareness of **'got'**, **'get'** and **'went'** being used, we can start to model to pupils the impact that these verbs can have and how we can actively make a significant impact by developing just one word. This will make children more empowered as authors.

Let's have a look at some examples. All of these examples are typical sentences that Age Related Expectations (ARE) pupils could write.

## 'Got' example

**I GOT out of bed.**

In this first example, '**I got out of bed**,' let's remember what we said about the cohesion of a sentence while keeping in mind the experience of the reader. Grammatically this sentence is fine and, as a one-off, there isn't really a problem. But when this happens too often, the problem is compounded and the experience the reader has is negatively impacted on. And as a writer, the next sentence feels more difficult to write because we are limiting our own inferences in the process.

Think about how you feel when you read the sentence, 'I got out of bed'. What does it make you feel, think and imagine? It feels unnatural, like the reader is being boxed in and prevented from inferring. If this happens sentence after sentence, then we will have a big problem.

**I RACED out of bed.**

**I AMBLED out of bed.**

**I CREPT out of bed.**

Now, if we look at the examples where '**got**' has been replaced by a more precise verb, all of a sudden, we have a dramatic change in the experience of the reader.

Think about how you feel when you read these sentences. Where does your mind automatically go? What subtle inferences do you subconsciously make about the character, their mood, their motivation and the setting they are in?

Hopefully you are already asking questions, thinking and making links to other knowledge without even realising you are doing it.

'**I raced out of bed.**' – Straight away, I'm thinking about the character and their sense of excitement and anticipation. Is it their birthday? Why are they getting out of bed so quickly? When did I act that way and why? I'm making links to my own life experiences: when I might have done this and how I felt at the time.

'**I stumbled out of bed.**' – What's happening? What happened the night before? Why are they so tired? What are they not looking forward to? Today may be tough for them. It's going to be a long day. They haven't got much energy. I'm making links to my own life experiences of when I might have done this and how I felt, as well as the texts and media I have read or watched.

'**I crept out of bed.**' – The character appears to be scared! Why? What's happening outside of the bedroom? Why are they being so quiet, as to creep? This helps us make links to other texts where characters have crept. These are normally spooky, thriller-type texts where tension is being built; normally the character is in some sort of danger. So, I'm making solid predictions and inferences based on the genre and text type.

Although these are just individual sentences, the more that we use them, the more we can start to build a far stronger sense of text development character and setting for the reader. Just three or four sentences using well-chosen verbs can transform a paragraph and create a vivid imagery for the reader.

By choosing these words and phrases, our pupils are showing their intent as authors. They are 'consciously manipulating' their vocabulary choices; this links directly to the 'At Expected Standard' (AES) and 'Greater Depth' (GD) sections of the Teacher Assessment Framework for writing.

## 'Get' example

**The team needed to GET another point.**

'**The team needed to get another point.**' – The use of 'get' in this sentence makes it feel quite limited and generic. Although it works – grammatically speaking – it isn't enjoyable to read.

We also need to be aware that we have just stated a fact because of the verb choice, which isn't particularly cohesive or engaging for the reader.

> The team needed to **SCORE** another point.
>
> The team needed to **FIGHT FOR** another point.

> We **WANDERED** to the park.
>
> We **SNUCK** to the park.
>
> We **SKIPPED** to the park.

**'The team needed to score another point.'** – The use of the verb 'score' immediately makes the reader think of a game, competition or sport. The team is currently getting beaten; is it the dying minutes of the game?

**'The team needed to fight for another point.'** – Within this example, 'fight for' makes it feel more extreme, even dangerous. There's a competitive battle between the two teams and it's going to be close. The other team are motivated to win too!

With these examples of 'get', we start to lean into developing the phrases 'fight for' or 'fight to the bitter end', not just as individual vocabulary choices. These are perfect for modelling to our ARE and GD writers, who will eagerly absorb and replicate these verb phrases.

**'Went' example**

> We **WENT** to the park.

**'We went to the park.'** – It's important to remind ourselves that we are not discounting this sentence or the use of went. This type of sentence might sit well among more complex and descriptive sentences from our more confident writers. But when this simple sentence is the staple sentence type of the young writer and the verb variation is limited, this type of sentence and verb choice is going to become a problem very quickly.

The alternatives present so many simpler and more complex inference opportunities.

**'We wandered to the park.'**, **'We snuck off to the park.'** and **'We skipped to the park.'** Each of these examples offer so many inferences and insights into the character's motives, intentions and mood, just by choosing one word differently.

As pupils become increasingly aware of their verb choices, we can increase modelling how to evolve the verb into a verb phrase when modelling writing.

**'We wandered to the park.'** could become:

'We wandered without a care to the park.' or 'We wandered in different directions to the park.'

'We snuck off to the park.' could become:

'We snuck off in the warm, summer shadows to the park.' or 'We snuck in the danger of the shadows to the park.' Both phrases change the mood and atmosphere of the sentence in completely different ways. One carefree and naive; the other perilous and dark.

'We skipped to the park.' could become:

'We skipped joyfully to the park.' or 'We skipped, hand in hand, to the park.'

Within the process, we are constantly making pupils aware that a verb becoming a verb phrase isn't always necessary or required, but it's possible. It's up to us as authors to decide where and when we deploy them, with the reader always at the forefront of our minds.

**Take a look at the Adventurous Alternatives section (page 76) for more resources about word choice.**

# GOT, GET AND WENT WORKSHOP

**Improve these sentences by replacing the words 'got', 'get' or 'went' with more interesting alternatives.**

Jenny and Fred got a new car after the crash.

_____

John went into the kitchen to get a snack.

_____

I got out of the car and went into the shops.

_____

The aeroplane took off from the runway and went to Southampton.

_____

The wind got stronger, louder and faster, so I went inside.

_____

All that Marcus wanted was a new stunt scooter, so his mum went and got him one.

_____

I've just got an ice cream from my aunt.

_____

After the long walk, the group went up the stairs and went to bed.

_____

The soldiers needed to get to the next muster point and get to cover.

_____

Could you get me some fruit?

_____

As the sun went down, Alex got colder and the roaring flames of his fire got smaller.

_____

# POWER OF THE WORD OF THE DAY

Verb poverty in children's vocabularies will lead to them overusing words like got, get, went and want. Many others too: big, small, happy, sad – and all of their friends. Nearly all of these words have alternatives that pupils should at least be considering using in their writing. But if they don't know them, how can they use them? This is why the Word of the Day is the perfect opportunity, along with your high-quality texts, to teach and model these high-quality and high-frequency verbs that children will likely encounter as they read, again and again!

## BANNING WORDS

A word of warning: when specifically focusing on replacing three or four words, is that it sounds like we are 'banning' these words. This is not the case. Over time, we want to build pupils' awareness of the role of the verb within a sentence and how choosing the right verb can make a huge difference to what we are writing.

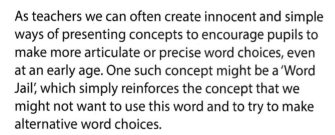

Take a look at the Scintillating Synonyms section (page 68) for more resources about verb choice.

As teachers we can often create innocent and simple ways of presenting concepts to encourage pupils to make more articulate or precise word choices, even at an early age. One such concept might be a 'Word Jail', which simply reinforces the concept that we might not want to use this word and to try to make alternative word choices.

Although the intentions are good, there are dangers in such concepts.

### Word Jail – a true cautionary tale!

In 2018, I oversaw a KS1 SATs reading paper where the reading text was called *Little Cousin Claire*. I noticed that a certain pupil was stuck on a specific question. Contextually, the pupil was an able reader and having read the paper beside pupils, it was obvious that the pupil should know the answer to the question they were on, and yet they had not moved beyond the question for around five minutes. The pupil in question was an able yet reluctant pupil and wasn't the type of pupil to ask for support but would instead rather just be stuck.

On approaching the pupil to ask if they were okay, they nodded in response. I quietly asked if they knew the answer and again they nodded. So I asked why they weren't writing the answer, if they knew it… Without a breath, the child pointed to the far wall and informed me that the answer was in the 'Word Jail' so they couldn't use it. Unbelievable!

The child was quickly reassured that it was okay to use this word as part of the reading paper and they continued without support.

To give some context, the word in question was 'blue'. The classroom teacher had used the Word Jail to encourage children to make alternative word choices to describe a beach setting within their writing. The intentions were good, just maybe the execution needed a little more thought. The word 'blue' was quite simply being overused as an adjective in the children's descriptions, but this child had taken the Word Jail far too literally.

The moral of the story is that we never want to 'ban' words, but rather consistently make pupils aware of the importance and impact of the words they choose within their writing.

## READING HIGH-QUALITY TEXTS ALOUD

By simply reading aloud to them, we can significantly expand any pupil's vocabulary. This links back to the finding of Hart and Risley (2003), who highlighted that 86 to 98 per cent of children's vocabularies at age three and four were developed due to the direct interactions with their parents – that is, hearing what their parents say, how they say it and the environment in which it is said. So, if we suppose that a child's vocabulary, at any age, will develop as a direct consequence of their exposure to their communication environment, then we must ensure that children hear the highest quality and richest vocabulary as often as possible.

### Benefits of reading aloud with pupils

**Expanded vocabulary:** Regular exposure through reading to a variety of words helps children to acquire a broader vocabulary. They are more likely to encounter new and diverse words that might not be part of their everyday conversations.

**Improved language skills:** Being read to enhances a child's language development. They learn about sentence structure, grammar and syntax, which are crucial components of effective communication. This exposure aids in the development of both receptive (understanding) and expressive (speaking) language skills.

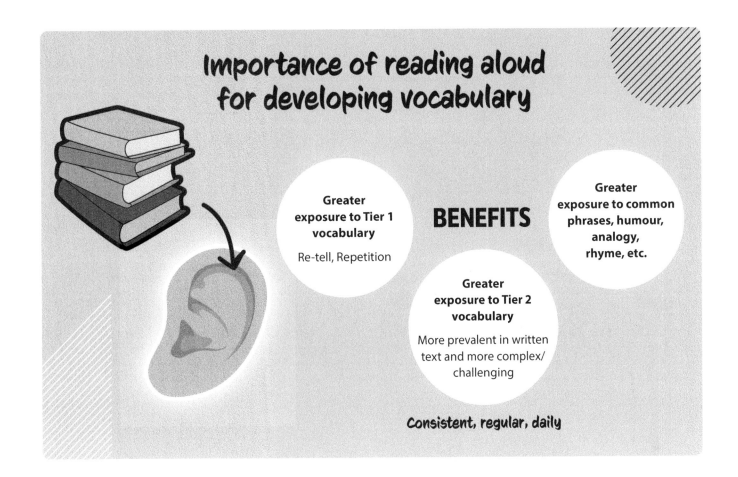

# Importance of reading aloud for developing vocabulary

**BENEFITS**

Greater exposure to Tier 1 vocabulary

Re-tell, Repetition

Greater exposure to common phrases, humour, analogy, rhyme, etc.

Greater exposure to Tier 2 vocabulary

More prevalent in written text and more complex/challenging

Consistent, regular, daily

---

**Enhanced cognitive skills:** Reading aloud stimulates cognitive development by encouraging active listening and concentration. Children engage with the storyline, follow characters and events, and comprehend the sequence of events. This cognitive engagement contributes to their overall intellectual growth.

**Better comprehension skills:** Exposure to varied stories and genres helps children to develop their comprehension skills. They learn to understand the meaning of words in context and grasp the nuances of different expressions. This skill is vital for academic success as they progress through school.

**Boosted communication skills:** Reading aloud encourages children to ask questions, express thoughts and engage in discussions about the story. This interactive process enhances their communication skills, including the ability to articulate ideas, ask for clarification and express themselves effectively.

As all Vocabulary Ninjas know, reading aloud to children has a profound impact on their vocabulary development, language skills, cognitive abilities, comprehension and overall communication skills. The positive effects extend beyond the immediate enjoyment of a story and contribute significantly to their educational and social development.

# PART 2
## VOCABULARY NINJA TEACHING TOOLKIT

Any ninja needs their tools. In this case, our tools are our vocabulary teaching resources. We have already begun to adopt a ninja mindset and evaluated our classroom effectiveness. We now need to arm ourselves with tried-and-tested resources that are guaranteed to bring vocabulary to life in the classroom.

So let's dive straight in and explore the resources!

# WORD OF THE DAY

This chapter is where your Word of the Day journey truly begins. It contains sample Grasshopper level words and sample Shinobi level words ready to use in the classroom.

Grasshopper and Shinobi words aren't about a level or status. As mentioned before, one child's 'huge' is another child's 'voracious'. Grasshopper words are simpler words that children are more likely to have heard before and, in most instances, will be simpler to apply. Thus, Grasshopper words tend to be used with children who have developing word pools, most likely our younger learners. I think it is important not to put an age on a word as it gives the message that it is only appropriate for some people to use it, and this is fundamentally wrong. Grasshopper words will often have a range of closely linked synonyms that make it much easier to understand and use. Shinobi words, on the other hand, may have a greater level of complexity that requires life experiences and grammatical understanding to not only comprehend them, but use them precisely. Shinobi words often have very few or no synonyms, and they have a very distinct purpose, meaning they can't just 'replace' a word as a Grasshopper word might be able to.

Each Word of the Day (WOD) comes complete with a comprehensive breakdown of the word. First and foremost, the WOD is split into syllables. Referencing the syllable count is often a great strategy to support spelling for pupils, so referring to this daily is extremely effective.

Each WOD is identified within a word class. Some may have two or three word classes that can be applied. For instance, a word may possibly be used as a noun, verb or adjective depending on its role within a sentence. It is crucial to discuss the word class with pupils, making clear the role the word plays within the sentence. The example sentence will only model the word in one context (as a verb, for instance), so it will certainly be good practice to be armed with another example that uses the word within a different word class – or at least be knowledgeable enough to discuss it further. This is why (as mentioned earlier in the book) subject knowledge is crucial when teaching vocabulary; it can be quite easy to become unstuck.

The definition comes next. The child-friendly definitions can make explaining the meaning of a word much easier. Often, when trying to define a word, children will use the target word over and over rather than explaining the meaning of the word. I would often say to pupils, 'Imagine the person you are talking to has never heard this word before. Simply saying the word you are trying to explain again and again won't help them understand.'

The definition is followed by the exemplar sentence with the target word in bold. The example sentences are often based around the school day or experiences that a child is likely to be familiar with, especially at Grasshopper level. Where possible, Shinobi-level words are pitched within a familiar context, but this isn't always the case. It's also important to note that the target word isn't always used in the same tense as it is presented at the top of the page. Words will often be used in varied tenses, which of course offers another important discussion point.

Pupils must understand that words can be manipulated and modified to suit the sentence they are creating. This leads nicely into the modifications identified at the bottom of the page. Synonyms and antonyms are great to discuss as they can often increase understanding through association to words that learners already understand. Prefix and suffix understanding is crucial to allow pupils to apply words in various tenses, with different meanings and correct spellings. Referring daily to spelling conventions linked to prefixes and suffixes is guaranteed to improve the accuracy of independent spelling.

All in all, the Word of the Day is a comprehensive resource designed to simplify and supercharge a small part of each teaching day.

# WORD OF THE DAY

## cover

| Word class: | noun or verb | Pronunciation: | cov-er |
|---|---|---|---|

| Definition: | If you **cover** something, you place something over it so that it can't be seen. |
|---|---|

| Example: | It's important to **cover** your mouth when you cough. |
|---|---|

| Synonym: | Antonym: | Prefix: | Suffix: |
|---|---|---|---|
| protect, shield | reveal | un-, re-, under- | -ed, -ing, -er |

Use the Word of the Day in a compound sentence.

# WORD OF THE DAY

## thought

| Word class: | noun | Pronunciation: | thought |
|---|---|---|---|

| Definition: | A **thought** is an idea from your mind. |
|---|---|

| Example: | Christopher has a **thought**, so he whispered it to Paola. |
|---|---|

| Synonym: | Antonym: | Prefix: | Suffix: |
|---|---|---|---|
| idea, notion | | after-, fore- | -ful, -less |

Use the Word of the Day in a single clause sentence.

# WORD OF THE DAY
## balance

| Word class: | noun or verb | Pronunciation: | bal-ance |
|---|---|---|---|

| Definition: | If you **balance** something, you place it so that it does not fall one way or the other. The weight is spread equally. |
|---|---|

| Example: | Emily **balanced** the apple on top of her head. |
|---|---|

| Synonym: | Antonym: | Prefix: | Suffix: |
|---|---|---|---|
|  | instability | im-, over-, un- | -ed, -ing, -er |

Use the Word of the Day in a compound sentence.

# WORD OF THE DAY

## adopt

| Word class: | verb | Pronunciation: | a-dopt |
|---|---|---|---|

| Definition: | If you **adopt** something, you make it your own. This could be a child, a mindset or a point of view. |
|---|---|

| Example: | The children had begun to **adopt** a more positive attitude towards their work. |
|---|---|

| Synonym: | Antonym: | Prefix: | Suffix: |
|---|---|---|---|
| embrace acquire | abandon | re- | -ed, -ing, -tion |

Use the Word of the Day in a single clause sentence.

Vocabulary Ninja © Andrew Jennings, 2024

# WORD OF THE DAY
## establish

| Word class: | verb | Pronunciation: | es-tab-lish |
|---|---|---|---|

| Definition: | If you **establish** something, you agree that it is true or have proof that shows it is true. |
|---|---|

| Example: | The evidence **established** his date of birth, which was previously unknown. |
|---|---|

| Synonym: | Antonym: | Prefix: | Suffix: |
|---|---|---|---|
| begin<br>initiate | demolish | dis-, re- | -ed, -ment, -ing |

Use the Word of the Day in a compound sentence.

---

# WORD OF THE DAY
## perish

| Word class: | verb | Pronunciation: | per-ish |
|---|---|---|---|

| Definition: | If something **perishes**, it is no longer alive or it no longer exists. |
|---|---|

| Example: | The vegetables **perished** during the drought. |
|---|---|

| Synonym: | Antonym: | Prefix: | Suffix: |
|---|---|---|---|
| expire<br>spoil | survive | | -ed, -ing, -able |

Use the Word of the Day in a question.

# WORD OF THE DAY
## measure

| Word class: | noun or verb | Pronunciation: | meas-ure |
|---|---|---|---|

| Definition: | If you **measure** something, you might identify how long, heavy or loud it is using a standard measure. |
|---|---|

| Example: | Paul's happiness could be **measured** by the number of coffees he has drunk that day. |
|---|---|

| Synonym: | Antonym: | Prefix: | Suffix: |
|---|---|---|---|
| weigh evaluate | estimate guess | counter-, re-, im- | -ed, -s, -ing |

Use the Word of the Day in a compound sentence.

# WORD OF THE DAY
## dwindle

| Word class: | verb | Pronunciation: | dwin-dle |
|---|---|---|---|

| Definition: | If something **dwindles**, it reduces in size or number. |
|---|---|

| Example: | Roger's energy showed no signs of **dwindling**. |
|---|---|

| Synonym: | Antonym: | Prefix: | Suffix: |
|---|---|---|---|
| reduce decrease | increase | | -ed, -ing |

Use the Word of the Day in a multi-clause sentence.

Vocabulary Ninja © Andrew Jennings, 2024

# ENTHRALLING ETYMOLOGY

This is a whole chapter dedicated to etymology and words that have interesting etymological stories to engage learners. Each of the words has a strong link to different parts of the curriculum. Plus, you'll find a bank of ideas about how to teach or use them in your already crammed curriculum.

Etymology was one of those words that was bandied around when I was an NQT. I would nod encouragingly in conversations but not really have any idea what it was. Etymology, in fact, is pretty awesome and is simply a scary name for something that is relatively straightforward: the study of where words came from.

The table on page 61 has almost 100 pertinent words for pupils to explore. All of these words have been chosen to link with topics across the curriculum. One of the great things about many of them is that they have some fabulously interesting stories behind them. The next few pages contain a wealth of ideas about how you might integrate the enthralling etymology strips into a lesson or your daily routine.

## NINJA GAME 1: SPEAKING AND LISTENING SLIPS

Speaking and listening opportunities can be hard to come by, especially in the middle of a busy English or science lesson. Using etymology slips can be a great way to provide a simple yet informative etymological speaking and listening opportunity.

**Prepare:** Simply pre-print a page of etymology explanations and slice them up, keeping the word and its definition together. Place the strips in an envelope and pin it onto your working wall.

**Pounce:** Whenever you have a spare two minutes or an opportunity to fill, ask pupils to pick a ninja word from the envelope and read it aloud to the rest of the class. This is a perfect assessment opportunity, but more importantly, their word pool is now a little deeper.

## NINJA GAME 2: MATCHING

Matching is a skill in itself and is especially important within reading comprehension. Pupils need to be able to match a word to its definition – quite simple really, or is it?

**Prepare:** Print a page and choose up to five words and associated explanations. Trim the word from the explanation about the origin of the word.

**Pounce:** First, present the words to the learners without the etymology. Ask them to hypothesise about the meaning of the word – what do they know about it already? Can they hear a root word held within it that might help them explain the word? All of this hypothesising will make the matching process much simpler. Now give the children the definitions. Can they match them together correctly? Alternatively, give the children the explanations first with the target word blanked out, then ask them to hypothesise about what the word might be.

## NINJA GAME 3: HANDWRITING

In a busy classroom environment, it's hard to fit everything in. Why not use etymology slips to teach the etymology of words and develop pupils' handwriting skills? Rather than simple copying worksheets, this is a meaningful handwriting activity that expands vocabulary.

**Prepare:** Print the etymology strips. Trim the slips and distribute them to pupils. To add an extra level of learning, give each table a different word and ask pupils to orally share the etymology with their peers. This creates an additional speaking and listening opportunity.

**Pounce:** Ask pupils to copy their word into their exercise books as neatly as they can. Ensure pupils have the chance to lay their books open, creating a handwriting gallery. Encourage pupils to move around and feed back to each other about the handwriting styles. To add an additional focus, be explicit about the handwriting element you want pupils to focus on, such as ascenders and descenders being formed correctly.

## NINJA GAME 4: TOPIC WORK

The majority of the etymology entries that have been provided have strong links to the primary National Curriculum, so they're perfect for topic and foundation subject lessons.

**Prepare:** Identify the vocabulary that supports your chosen topic and be ready to introduce it to the children.

**Pounce:** Use a relevant word and its etymology as a starter to each topic lesson. Have the etymology of the chosen word displayed on your interactive whiteboard or wall display and share it with the children. Think about how you can record this in a way that adds value. Could you have topic etymology books, where pupils record the etymology of the words? Why not finish with a quiz at the end of the year? Why not embed ICT skills? Suggest the pupils create an etymology blog that can be posted on the school's website or social media!

# NINJA GAME 5: ILLUSTRATE AN ETYMOLOGY FLOOR BOOK

Illustrations and drama activities can be fantastically engaging for pupils and can help to aid recall.

**Prepare:** I don't need to tell you about setting up a drawing activity, but we need to think about how we record this fantastic activity. Sometimes it won't be appropriate to record this in your foundation subject books.

**Pounce:** A great solution to this is to create a scrapbook or floor book and create a page for each word that you introduce to your class. Drop the etymology onto the page, then add examples of pupils' illustrations and thoughts about the word etymology itself.

# NINJA GAME 6: GREEN SCREEN

This is another fabulous opportunity for speaking and listening and the associated assessment. Green screens quickly engage pupils and are an effective medium for sharing the pupils' learning. Ask pupils to present the new information as a news report with a superimposed image that is related to the etymology of the chosen word.

**Prepare:** First, you will require a tablet or smartphone that can download a green screen recording app. There are several simple yet effective ones available for free. For a small fee, you can access versions with more features to enhance the outcomes. Second, you will need a wall space where you can hang green cloth or even cover the wall in green backing paper. It helps if this area is fairly well lit.

**Pounce:** Once you have the area prepared and have familiarised yourself with the app, you are ready to go. Just make sure the pupils aren't wearing green too! Display an image that illustrates the target word and its etymology, and invite the children to present their new learning.

# NINJA GAME 7: FIVE-SENTENCE STORY

Five-sentence stories can be extremely entertaining and can provide a great insight into pupils' strengths in writing. Five-sentence stories are exactly what you might think they are: stories that are limited to five sentences. They can take the structure of your traditional story mountain and be as simple or as complex as a child can make them. Just add imagination.

**Prepare:** Modelling your very own five-sentence story would be a great place to start, showing the pupils exactly what you expect, using the etymology of the new word as an inspiration for the story. For example, if you have just introduced the etymology of the word 'buccaneer', that would be a great inspiration for a pirate or adventure story around Caribbean islands.

**Pounce:** Ask the children to create their own five-sentence stories using an etymology as inspiration.

# NINJA GAME 8: TELL-A-TEACHER CHALLENGE

The tell-a-teacher challenge is a fabulous tool for spreading knowledge and understanding, which encourages pupils to use their communication skills with other adults.

**Prepare:** Introduce the new etymology to the children, then set the mission. 'Your mission, if you choose to accept it, is to tell as many adults in the school during break and lunch about the etymology of this new word! Good luck.'

**Pounce:** Model some of the language that pupils might use, e.g. 'Excuse me Miss/Sir, do you know the etymology of the word buccaneer?' This will give pupils the confidence to approach other adults across the school. It would be prudent to inform your colleagues that pupils will be approaching staff to share their new learning. Who can tell the most adults during break and lunch?

# NINJA GAME 9: THE LITTLE BOOK OF ETYMOLOGY

A small book of enormous words! Decide whether you want to create a whole-class book or individual pupil books. Personally, I think individual books have a more intimate feel.

**Prepare:** Give pupils small books or booklets. Invite them to decorate them or even back them in wallpaper (very 90s).

**Pounce:** Every time you introduce a new etymology to the children, ask them to record the entry in their Little Book of Etymology. They could add images, definitions, associated topics and even sketches to bring the etymology to life.

# ENTHRALLING ETYMOLOGY

| Word | Etymology |
|------|-----------|
| **Amazon** | From the Greek *Amazones* (a tribe of war-fighting women) who were dangerous and brutal. As you can imagine, the Amazon River isn't for the faint hearted! |
| **armada** | 'Fleet of warships', from Medieval Latin *armata* meaning 'armed force'. The Spanish Armada was the allegedly invincible fleet sent by Philip II of Spain to defeat England in 1588. |
| **artery** | This word comes from the Latin and Greek word *arteria*, which means 'windpipe'. The arteries were originally thought to carry air throughout the body. |
| **assassin** | Members of a Muslim sect during the Crusades who murdered leaders on the opposing side. Their enemies used the word 'hashishiyyin', meaning smokers of hashish (i.e. drug-takers) to discredit them, and through centuries of mispronunciation, English arrived at this word. |
| **battery** | This word originates from Old French *baterie*, meaning 'beating, thrashing, assault'. In the 1550s, the French began to use the word to describe artillery units, which discharged explosives towards the enemy walls. In the same sense, during the 1790s, it began to mean the 'electrical cell' created by Benjamin Franklin, which discharged electricity much like the artillery. |
| **berserk** | This word, in its literal Scandinavian sense, is a 'raging warrior of superhuman strength'. |
| **bonfire** | This word has an uncertain past, although most people concede that it has an original meaning of 'bone fire'. |
| **boycott** | This word comes from when Irish tenant farmers ostracised the English land agent Captain Charles Boycott because he refused to lower the rent for them. This was quickly adopted by newspapers in many languages, even as far as Japan: 'boikotto'. |
| **breakfast** | This is usually the first meal of the day. During the night your body is considered to be in a mode called 'fasting' or in a 'fast'. You might 'break' or stop your fast in the morning. |
| **bubo** | This word means 'inflamed swelling in the glands' and originates from the 14th century and the bubonic plague. |
| **buccaneer** | This word emerged in the 17th century, originating from the French word *boucanier*, which meant 'a pirate; a curer of wild meats, a user of a *boucan*', a native grill for roasting meat. |
| **burrow** | Meaning a 'hole in the ground dug by an animal as a refuge or to live in', the word stems from *borewe* which comes from Old English *burgh* meaning a 'stronghold or fortress'. |
| **bus** | Originally an abbreviation of *omnibus*, meaning 'four-wheeled public vehicle with seats for passengers'. |

# ENTHRALLING ETYMOLOGY

| Word | Etymology |
|---|---|
| **careless** | This word is an old English word meaning 'unconcerned'. |
| **carnation** | Most people, when they think of this word, picture a flower. But before it was used to describe a flower, it was used to refer to the pink colour of skin. |
| **caterpillar** | From the Middle English *piller* 'plunderer', from Late Latin *catta pilosa*, where *catta* meant 'hairy, shaggy, covered with hair'. |
| **centipede** | Venomous, many-legged, insect-sized arthropod, from French *centipède*, from Latin *centipeda* 'many-footed arthropod', from *centum* 'hundred' and *ped* meaning 'foot', so literally meaning 100 feet. |
| **checkmate** | This term, beloved by chess grand masters, comes from the Arabic *shah mat*, meaning 'the king died' or the Persian *shah mat*, meaning 'the king is helpless'. |
| **chocolate** | The Nahuatl *xocolatl* is made up of the parts *xococ*, meaning 'bitter', and *atl*, meaning 'water'. |
| **clue** | This word means 'anything that serves as a guide or aid in a task or problem'. According to Greek mythology, when Theseus entered the Labyrinth to kill the minotaur (a half-man, half-bull), he unraveled a 'clew' (a ball of string) behind him, so he could find his way back. |
| **codpiece** | A bagged appendage to the front of close-fitting breeches, from Old English *codd* 'a bag, pouch, husk' which in Middle English came to mean 'testicle'. |
| **conspire** | From Old French *conspirer*, from Latin meaning literally 'to breathe together'. |
| **courage** | This word is similar to 'bravery'. It is from the Old French word *curage*, which draws from the word *cuer*, meaning 'heart'. |
| **cure** | From Old French *curer* and Latin *curare* 'take care of', hence in medical language 'to treat'. |
| **cycle** | From Greek *kyklos* meaning 'circle, wheel, any circular body, circular motion or cycle of events'. |
| **daisy** | The flower. This word is actually a contraction of 'day's eye' because the flower opens in the morning and closes at night! |
| **dam** | Meaning 'barrier across a stream of water to obstruct its flow and raise its level', this word is probably from Old Norse *dammr* or Middle Dutch *dam*. Reinforced by Old English verb *fordemman* meaning 'to stop up, block'. |
| **dandelion** | From Old French *dent de lion* 'lion's tooth' (from its toothed leaves). |
| **diary** | From Latin *diarium* meaning 'daily allowance'. All origins and derivatives seem to relate to 'day', showing that an entry was to be made daily. |

# ENTHRALLING ETYMOLOGY

| Word | Etymology |
|------|-----------|
| **dinosaur** | This word was coined in Modern Latin by Sir Richard Owen, from Greek *deinos* 'terrible' plus *sauros* 'lizard'. The word is sometimes used to describe 'a person or institution not adapting to change'. |
| **disaster** | This word comes from the Greek *dis* meaning 'bad', and *astron*, meaning 'star'. The Ancient Greeks used to blame calamities on unfavourable planetary positions. |
| **eavesdrop** | This word means 'to lurk near a place to hear what is said inside'. It comes from Old English *yfesdrype*, 'a place around a house where the rainwater drips off the roof'. |
| **echo** | This word means 'a sound repeated by reflection'. In classical mythology, there was a mountain nymph who was punished with a speech problem that meant she could only repeat the words of others. |
| **erupt** | This word originally came about in relation to the breakout of diseases. It comes from Latin *eruptus* meaning 'to break out, burst'. For volcanoes, the Latin word was actually used when talking about Mount Etna. |
| **extinct** | This word means 'extinguished, quenched', from Latin *extinctus/exstinctus*, meaning 'to put out, quench; go out, die out; kill, destroy'. It is commonly used to describe a species of animal that has died out. |
| **extinguish** | From Latin *extinguere* meaning to 'quench or put out (what is burning)'. From *ex-* for 'out' and *stinguere* for 'quench'. |
| **factory** | This word is a place where different processes are done or objects are made. The related word *factor* in Latin meant a 'doer or maker'. |
| **flood** | An Old English *flōd* was 'a flowing of water, tide, an overflowing of land by water, a deluge, Noah's Flood; mass of water, river, sea, wave'. In early modern English, it was often called a *floud*. In figurative use it can mean, 'a great quantity, a sudden abundance'. |
| **genocide** | A term used to describe violence against members of a national, ethnical, racial or religious group with the intent to destroy the entire group. The word was apparently coined in 1944 in reference to the Nazi extermination of Jewish people, literally 'killing a tribe', from Greek *genos* 'race, kind' and *-cide* 'a killing'. |
| **geography** | 'The science of description of the earth's surface', from Greek *geographia*, 'description of the earth's surface' from *geo-* meaning 'earth' and *-graphia* meaning 'description'. |
| **ghoul** | A legendary evil spirit that robs graves and feeds on corpses. The word comes from the Arabic *ghūl* (which is itself from *ghāla*, meaning 'to seize'). |
| **glacier** | This word is from Old French *glace*, meaning 'ice'. |
| **greenhouse** | This word is called this simply because it is a transparent house and all of the produce within is normally green. |

# ENTHRALLING ETYMOLOGY

| Word | Etymology |
|------|-----------|
| **groggy** | This word means 'drunk, overcome with grog'. The word *grog* originated in the 18th century when a British Admiral was nicknamed 'Old Grog' because he wore a cloak made of *grogram*. The Admiral made sailors dilute their rum with water to make a mixture called *grog*. |
| **hammer** | Originally meaning 'stone tool', this word comes from Old English *hamor*. |
| **hamstring** | This word means 'the tendon at the back of the knee'. When the thighs of pigs (hams) were hung by butchers, they were hung through the string-like tendons of these muscles. |
| **hazard** | This word means 'danger or risk'. It comes from Old French *hasard, hasart* meaning 'game of chance played with dice'. |
| **hero** | This word means 'a man of superhuman strength or physical courage' and has close links to *hērōs* (Greek) meaning 'demi-god'. |
| **hippopotamus** | This word literally means 'river horse' in Greek. It might not look much like a horse, but it certainly lives in rivers. |
| **holocaust** | The word comes from the Greek word *holokauston* which refers to an animal sacrifice that is offered to a god in which the whole animal is completely burnt. Later it came to denote a massacre of large numbers of people. |
| **hopscotch** | This is a well-known children's game. The word combines *hop* and *scotch*, the latter which means 'scratch', from the lines scored in the dirt to make the squares for the game. |
| **hospital** | This word comes from Late Latin *hospitale* originally meaning 'guest-house, inn'. The meaning became 'an institution for sick or wounded people' in the 1540s. |
| **inspire** | This word comes from *enspiren* meaning 'to fill (the mind, heart with grace)' and before that from Latin *inspirare* meaning 'blow into or breathe upon'. |
| **Kilimanjaro** | This is a mountain in Tanzania, Africa. It may originate from *Swahili kilima*, meaning '(little) mountain'. |
| **knight** | This word comes from Old English *cniht* meaning 'boy, youth, servant'. As time passed, this work became closely linked to a military servant or follower of the king. Finally it become a noble rank in the 16th century. |
| **ladybird** | This word originated in Britain where the insects became known as Our Lady's Bird instead of 'ladybug' as they were known elsewhere. 'Lady' means Mary, so these insects were Mary's birds/bugs. |
| **lemur** | The animal received its name from Latin. In Roman mythology, the plural 'lemures' was used to describe the evil spirits of the dead. |
| **London** | This word appeared in Latin as *Londinium*. By the first century CE, this was a commercial centre in Roman Britain. |

# ENTHRALLING ETYMOLOGY

| Word | Etymology |
|------|-----------|
| **Luftwaffe** | This German word literally means 'air-weapon'. The first part, *Luft*, is linked to 'loft', meaning go high in the air. |
| **lunatic** | This word is from Late Latin *lunaticus* meaning 'moon-struck'. This originated from the belief that insanity was caused by changes of the moon! |
| **malaria** | This word originates from Italy. It combines *mal* 'bad' and *aria* 'air', so it literally means 'bad air'. The term was used to describe the unpleasant air emanating from the marshlands of Rome, which was believed to cause the disease. |
| **Matterhorn** | One of the world's most famous mountains, it has taken its name from its surroundings and appearance: *Matte* in German meaning 'meadow, pastureland' and *horn* from its horn-like shape. |
| **million** | A mathematical word for you to think about. From Italian *milione* meaning 'a great thousand'. It is interesting to note that the ancient Greeks didn't have a name for a number larger than ten thousand, and the Romans for none higher than a hundred thousand. |
| **Mississippi** | This is now the name of a state, but originally it was the name of the river running through it. The word comes from the French rendering of an Algonquian name meaning 'big river'; compare Ojibwa *mshi-* 'big' and *ziibi* 'river'. |
| **moat** | This word originated from the French *mote* meaning a 'hillock, mound or embankment' – quite the opposite of what we consider to be a moat today! In Norman times the meaning shifted when ditches were dug around castles to protect them. |
| **mortgage** | This word comes from the Old French *mort* 'dead' and *gage* 'pledge', and now I don't want to buy a house anymore! |
| **naughty** | This word originally meant 'having nothing', from *nought* and -y, but was also used to describe people having no morals. |
| **nemesis** | Today this word means mortal enemy. It is also the name of the Greek goddess who took revenge against those who showed arrogance before the gods. |
| **orangutan** | This word for an animal comes from the Malay *orang*, meaning 'person', and *hutan*, meaning 'forest' – so 'person of the forest'. |
| **periscope** | Viewing apparatus on a submarine, 1899, formed in English from *peri* meaning 'around' and -*scope* meaning 'instrument for viewing'. So the word means 'an instrument for looking around'. |
| **phobia** | This word means 'irrational fear, horror, aversion' and comes from Greek *phobos*. Phobos is the son of the Greek god Ares. |
| **pirate** | This word comes from Latin *pirata* meaning 'sailor, sea robber'. |

# ENTHRALLING ETYMOLOGY

| Word | Etymology |
|------|-----------|
| **plastic** | From the 1630s, this word means 'capable of shaping or molding', from Latin *plasticus*, from Greek *plastikos* meaning 'able to be molded, pertaining to molding, fit for molding'. |
| **protect** | This word comes from the Latin *protectus*, past participle of *protegere*. The word is made of *pro* meaning 'before' and *tegere* meaning 'to cover'. |
| **Pterodactyl** | An extinct flying reptile. This word comes originally from Greek *pteron* 'wing' and *daktylos* 'finger'. |
| **python** | This word is the name of the enormous dragon-like serpent that was slain by the legendary hero Apollo. The site of its death was known as *Pytho* to the Ancient Greeks. |
| **quarantine** | This word used to mean the 'period a ship suspected of carrying disease is kept in isolation', from Italian *quarantina giorni*, literally 'space of forty days'. During the days of the Black Death, ships suspected of carrying the plague were not allowed to enter Venetian ports for a period of 40 days. |
| **ransack** | From the Old Norse *rannsaka* 'to pillage', literally 'search the house' (especially legally, for stolen goods). |
| **rhinoceros** | This word literally means 'nose-horned', from Greek *rhinokeros* where rhinos means 'nose' and *keras* means 'horn of an animal'. |
| **Russia** | Vikings who travelled east and settled in Kyiv in the ninth century were known as *Rus*. |
| **salary** | The word salary comes from the Latin *salarium*, said to be a soldier's allowance for the purchase of salt. In ancient times, salt was used for many important things, and was referred to as white gold. Used as an antiseptic, a preservative and as payment. |
| **sarcasm** | It is descended ultimately from the late Greek sarkasmos 'a sneer, jest, taunt, mockery', from *sarkazein* meaning literally 'to strip off the flesh'. |
| **segregate** | From Latin *segregare* meaning to 'set apart, lay aside; isolate; divide', literally 'separate from the flock'. |
| **shark** | A large fish with lots of varieties, e.g. great white and hammerhead. The origin of the name for these animals is under some debate, but the English word may be from a Mayan word, *xoc*. Northern Europeans seem not to have been familiar with these animals before voyages to the tropics began. |
| **shelter** | This word is possibly an alteration of Middle English *sheltron, sheldtrume* meaning 'roof or wall formed by locked shields'. You can imagine soldiers holding shields aloft in the air, joined together to protect the group from arrows or other enemy attacks. |
| **shield** | This word comes from the Old English *scield* meaning 'protect, defence' and in a more literal sense 'board'. |

# ENTHRALLING ETYMOLOGY

| Word | Etymology |
|------|-----------|
| shrapnel | This word was the surname of a general who invented a type of exploding, fragmenting shell when he was a lieutenant in the Royal Artillery during the Peninsular War. These days the word is sometimes used to refer to small change in purses or pockets. |
| snail | This word essentially is a diminutive form of Old English *snaca* 'snake', which literally means 'creeping thing'. |
| sniper | Another word for a sharpshooter. This word was used in 1773 by British soldiers in India to describe shooting from a hidden place. It is a reference to hunting snipe (a type of small bird) as game. |
| sunflower | It is suggested this flower was given its name due to its similarity to the sun itself! |
| Thames | This is the name for the river running through London. It is thought that the name comes from Old English *Temese*, from Latin *Tamesis* (51 BCE), from British *Tamesa*, an ancient Celtic river name perhaps meaning 'the dark one'. |
| Thursday | The fifth day of the week. The name for this day stems from Old English *þurresdæg*, literally 'Thor's Day', who was the Norse god of thunder. |
| titanic | This word is derived from the word *titan* meaning 'gigantic, colossal'. The word was the name of a British passenger liner which sank in 1912, and the word became symbolic of the destruction of the supposedly indestructible. |
| tsunami | This word is from Japanese – *tsu* 'harbour' and *nami* 'waves'. |
| typhoon | There are a few fascinating possible stories for this word. One favourite is from Greek *typhon*, meaning 'whirlwind'. It was personified as a father of the winds, a giant. Interestingly, the Arabic word *al-tufan* appears many times in the Qur'an to mean 'a flood or storm'. |
| Tyrannosaurus Rex | A large, carnivorous dinosaur that walked on two legs. Its name is from the Greek *tyrannos* 'tyrant' and *sauros* 'lizard', and the Latin *rex* 'king'. |
| Victoria | This woman's name means 'victory in war' in Latin, and is the name of the Roman goddess of victory. |
| volcano | This word stems from the name Vulcan, the Roman God of fire. The Romans actually believed that Vulcan's workshop was based at the foot of Mt. Etna. |
| whipping-boy | In Tudor times, wealthy families would often pay for a 'whipping-boy' if their child misbehaved. The whipping-boy received physical punishment instead of the rich child! |
| window | Translated literally from Old Norse, this word means 'wind eye'. It stems from *vindauga*, where *vindr* means *wind* and *auga* is *eye*. |
| yeti | This word comes from the Sherpa (Tibetan) word *yeh-teh*, meaning a 'small humanlike animal'. |

# SCINTILLATING SYNONYMS

Understanding synonyms can be a terrific way of expanding pupils' vocabulary, developing their spelling, punctuation and grammar knowledge, and can help to refine the incisiveness of their writing. As we have discussed earlier in the book, pupils can only use the words they hold within their working vocabulary, which is influenced by their environment. For nearly every pupil, the three environments they are exposed to are: home, school and unstructured environments.

The three models opposite illustrate the effect that social factors can have on the width and depth of a pupil's vocabulary. Pupils who have enriched experiences in all three environments are much more likely to have a more expansive vocabulary that filters through all aspects of their lives. The central part of each model is the vocabulary that is deeply embedded – vocabulary that pupils can draw upon and use effectively within any environment.

Notice the dashed external boundary to our vocabulary pool. Within the rich model, our word pools are being forced to expand as our environments expose us to more rich and varied language experiences. However, within the impoverished model, pupils' word pools aren't necessarily expanding, and they also have the potential to recede. The embedded language that is cross-environmental is also limited. Within this model, we can see how the school environment is crucial and, in most instances, is the only environment we can reasonably expect to control.

We want to ensure, where possible, that pupils' working oral and written vocabularies are expanding, growing and deepening at all times. As Vocabulary Ninjas, we can ensure that this happens for all pupils. It's logical to expect, for those pupils whose home and social environments are stimulating and enriched, that their experimental and embedded word pools will be growing at a much quicker rate. The rich/poor model illustrates the school environment as an enriched one. Yes, the pupils still have limited rich language experiences outside of the school environment, but school can make the difference – *you* can make the difference. For these pupils, the school environment is fighting the great fight, pushing and expanding the external boundary on its own. It's tough going it alone, but if the school environment doesn't do it, who will?

So, let's look at how synonyms can be the infantry troops of our word army, as we try to expand our territories and take over the world! (Wait… did I say that last part out loud?)

## DEVELOPING LONG-TERM VOCABULARY SKILLS

Synonyms can be as simple or as complex as required. The potential danger with synonyms is that they can be used in an extremely superficial manner if you don't dedicate the time to embedding pupils' understanding. The classic example of this can be found in an episode of *Friends* (the popular television sitcom from the 90s). Joey, one of the main characters, is trying to write a letter but is not competent enough to do so, and so is introduced to the thesaurus facility on his computer. He proceeds to swap out nearly every word in his letter for a 'better' one with disastrous, yet hilarious, consequences. This is a terrific proxy for how synonyms are used within the classroom.

As teachers, the danger is that we offer children words in a word bank or use an exciting scaffold that goes down well in an observation but really, they have only been supported superficially. Offering words up as alternatives is great practice, but I want to dive deeper into pupils' understanding.

> 'Give a man a fish and he won't go hungry today. Teach him to fish, and he will never go hungry again' is the old adage. The same is true with our teaching of synonyms and alternative vocabulary (or any learning). Give our pupils a word bank and they will use it today – superficially. Teach them how, and why, and which word choices to make (supported by the word bank if required) and they will use those word choices incisively every day.

### COLOSSAL FISH AND CHIPS

If synonyms are to be our foot soldiers – the first line of attack and defence, against repetition and the mundane – then they need to be disciplined, highly trained and deployed effectively by the Grand Master.

# THREE MODELS OF VOCABULARY

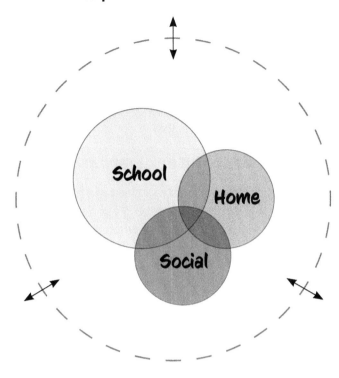

**Impoverished environments**

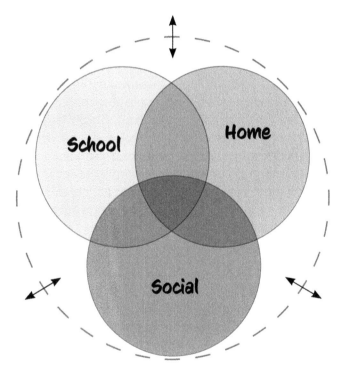

**Rich environments**

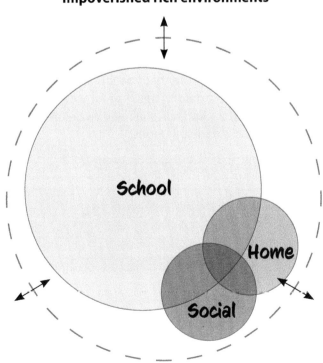

**Impoverished rich environments**

For our youngest grasshoppers, it is certainly more appropriate for pupils to be made aware that there are lots of words in our language and that they can mean the same thing as each other or have very similar meanings. As pupils become older, we must introduce a variety of synonyms of increasing complexity. Depending on the context in which they are used, certain words may no longer be appropriate synonyms. For example, there are many ways to say 'big', and although 'big' and 'colossal' are synonyms, I wouldn't want pupils just replacing 'big' with 'colossal' at every opportunity. If this starts to happen, synonyms can quickly become a literary quicksand learners become trapped by. We must dangle the vines from our vocabulary jungle and drag our pupils from its grasp, setting them free.

It is important that pupils understand that we are not just blindly replacing one word for another; sometimes the teaching or introduction of synonyms by teachers implies that this is true or possible. *'Synonyms are words that mean the same thing.'* Yes, this is true. But – and this is a significant but – this is wholly dependent on the context in which they are being used. For example, if a pupil was eating a 'big sandwich', they might be eating a sandwich that is larger than their friend's sandwich or possibly larger in size than expected. Whereas, a 'colossal sandwich' might suggest that it is not only a much larger sandwich than expected, but also implies that it is of much greater quality and has more ingredients within the sandwich. (Maybe a ripe gherkin or two, with some continental meats and a carefully selected sauce-based condiment.)

Another food-related example: a 'big bag of fish and chips'. What about a 'colossal bag of fish and chips'? These do not mean the same thing. What does a big bag of fish and chips suggest? In my mind, a big bag of fish and chips means it wasn't the smallest available and that there is a decent amount of chips and a good-sized piece of fish, nothing more. However, if you say 'a colossal bag of fish and chips', I see chips overflowing from the wrapper, an enormous fish with crispy batter, and salt and vinegar permeating the wrapped paper. There's no way you'll eat them all. It's a bag of chips to be savoured, a bag that will be talked about in weeks and months to come.

The point being made is that even though 'big' and 'colossal' are synonyms that denote how large a subject or object is, we must ensure that pupils begin to understand the subtle differences (the alternative meaning) that each synonym offers. Within the two food-based examples, we can quickly see how a pupil's skilled deployment of such words can help them add meaning and depth to a description, a conversation or a piece of writing. It will also add meaning when they read. The images that they will be able to build within their own mind will be subtler, more vivid and more enjoyable.

## NOT SYNONYMS, RATHER... ALTERNATIVES

At this stage, it is important to understand that 'big' is a great word – there isn't anything wrong with 'big'. 'Big' only becomes a big problem when it is used as an adjective to describe *everything*. The pupils who are most likely to do this are the pupils who sit in the impoverished word pool model, and to a lesser degree the pupils who are found in the rich/poor word pool model.

In order to set them free, pupils need to understand the subtle differences of each word; we also want pupils to think carefully about what they are trying to say, i.e. what they are trying to accomplish by using that word. It should come as no surprise that this will require teaching and, more importantly, modelling. Learners must see examples, experiment, make mistakes, discuss their ideas and refine their understanding. We want older pupils to be able to use each word with meaning. To do this, they must understand the context they are trying to use the word in. By understanding that 'colossal' is a great *alternative* to 'big', rather than a synonym, pupils can start to make more meaningful and incisive word choices. Try offering words to pupils as *alternatives*, instead of synonyms.

N.B. It is important to note that Vocabulary Ninja is not asserting that you shouldn't teach synonyms. This aspect of the curriculum will still need to be taught and understood clearly by pupils.

> It is important that teachers use the correct technical language with pupils. If *you* don't know (be honest), how can we expect the pupils to? #SubjectKnowledge
>
> NINJA NOTES

Especially within writing, I wouldn't hesitate to say that the increasing prominence of the SPaG curriculum and testing systems hasn't been particularly helpful. It is very mechanical. Synonyms are quite mechanical. If we just see them as one thing that simply replaces another, it implies that we have no freedom or control. It implies that there is no need for personal thoughts or creativity. And, because SPaG can be taught quite mechanically, the quicksand can once again take hold of our creativity and reduce it down to a box to be ticked. We have to avoid this at all costs.

The next resource is an effective way of diving a little deeper into the subtle differences between words. The resource applies the synonyms within the same sentence – very similar to the fish and chips example – so that learners can see for themselves why a synonym might not work. 'Hate' and 'detest' would be considered strong synonyms with each other. However, hate and detest have subtle differences in their definitions and meanings; we cannot just swap one for the other blindly and assert that the same meaning is implied.

# SCINTILLATING SYNONYMS

| Words | hate (verb) | detest (verb) |
|---|---|---|
| Context | The children <u>hate</u> peas. | The children <u>detest</u> peas. |
| Definition | If you hate someone or something, you have a strong feeling of dislike for them. | If you detest someone or something, you dislike them with extreme negative emotion. |
| Difference | In the context of peas and children, hate is offering up a dislike, common to children; something they might say but they could still be coaxed to eat them. However, if the children detest the peas, this is a much stronger feeling; perhaps they have caused illness previously, which the children remember.<br><br>In this example, detest offers a more potent dislike of the peas.<br><br>The children hate peas, <u>but still ate them</u>.<br><br>The children detest peas, <u>so the peas had to be scraped from the plate</u>. | |

# SCINTILLATING SYNONYMS

| Words | love (verb) | treasure (verb) | idolise (verb) |
|---|---|---|---|
| Context | I <u>love</u> this band. | I <u>treasure</u> this band. | I <u>idolise</u> this band. |
| Definition | | | |
| Difference | | | |

# SCINTILLATING SYNONYMS

| Words | | |
|---|---|---|
| Context | | |
| Definition | | |
| Difference | | |

# SCINTILLATING SYNONYMS

| Words | | | |
|---|---|---|---|
| Context | | | |
| Definition | | | |
| Difference | | | |

# SYNONYM MATCHING PAIR CARD GAME

| alike | lethargic | old | tropical | mature |
|---|---|---|---|---|
| assist | hot | lazy | similar | help |

| relocate | new | strong | delightful | mighty |
|---|---|---|---|---|
| sad | charming | move | modern | glum |

| pink | green | charcoal | marmalade | mustard |
|---|---|---|---|---|
| yellow | orange | salmon | emerald | black |

# SYNONYM MATCHING PAIR CARD GAME

| | | | | |
|---|---|---|---|---|
| thrilled | excited | tearful | intrepid | fearful |
| unhappy | scared | brave | happy | ecstatic |

| | | | | |
|---|---|---|---|---|
| cold | dark | brave | freezing | wretched |
| bad | angry | irritated | murky | daring |

| | | | | |
|---|---|---|---|---|
| amazing | love | famous | pretty | frolic |
| beautiful | play | splendid | cherish | popular |

# ADVENTUROUS ALTERNATIVES

As discussed throughout the book, children often don't intentionally make poor or repetitive word choices. Quite simply, they have no other choice. As a teacher, you will have read thousands and thousands of pieces of pupils' writing and the same words will crop up over and over again. Once again, we must think about why this is happening and so, quite simply, the children have no alternatives within their working word bank to draw upon. Words such as 'good', 'bad', 'happy' and 'sad' are far too common for Vocabulary Ninja's liking!

Vocabulary Ninja has endeavoured to provide alternatives for these nuisance words. In the Adventurous Alternatives resource, you'll find 101 commonly overused words and 606 alternatives. The words in the far-left column are words that, as teachers, you will see and hear used all of the time. Pupils overuse these words because they have no other alternatives within their repertoire. This resource gives pupils a range of alternatives to use within their writing. When using such a resource, it's important to ensure that the words from the left column are not seen as words that we can't use. The only reason why we want to use alternatives for these words is that they are generally used in an overly repetitive

manner. For example, not everything is 'bad' – bad isn't always the most appropriate word choice, though sometimes it will be. We want pupils to understand, use and remember alternatives for these sometimes troublesome words.

Each alternative word has been ranked from Grasshopper to Grand Master (for fun – there is some level of increasing complexity, but not always). So, 606 pieces of prepared language for pupils to use, laid out in a way that can be simply photocopied and trimmed. These words may be contextually different, meaning that they are not necessarily synonyms; it all depends on the context in which they are found and used.

All of the words found here are ideal to explore using the Vocabulary laboratory resources sheet on page 84. Remember, a list alone is only so useful – we need to go all out ninja on each word to explore it, explain it, break it down, give it meaning in context. Eventually, your learners will become more ninja and do this for themselves.

# ADVENTUROUS ALTERNATIVES

| Grasshopper | Shinobi | Warrior | Samurai | Assassin | Grand Master |
|---|---|---|---|---|---|
| fantastic | incredible | remarkable | splendid | staggering | breathtaking |
| cross | fuming | annoyed | irritated | irate | exasperated |
| spectacular | glorious | astonishing | exceptional | sensational | phenomenal |
| awful | rotten | dreadful | wretched | vile | loathsome |
| appealing | elegant | enticing | angelic | ravishing | bewitching |
| large | vast | immense | oversized | mammoth | gargantuan |
| ink | soot | charcoal | onyx | pitch | ebony |
| navy | sky | denim | peacock | teal | azure |
| dull | dreary | repetitive | tedious | monotonous | wearisome |
| heroic | daring | gutsy | intrepid | courageous | gallant |
| crack | smash | wreck | shatter | fracture | obliterate |
| wood | coffee | penny | chocolate | mocha | gingerbread |
| freezing | chilly | bitter | biting | arctic | sub-zero |
| arrive | near | join | reach | approach | advance |
| scream | weep | sob | bawl | yowl | whimper |
| unsafe | risky | perilous | hazardous | dicey | treacherous |
| dim | dusky | gloomy | murky | shaded | sunless |
| wreck | damage | impair | shatter | ravage | annihilate |
| taxing | demanding | challenging | exhausting | strenuous | back breaking |
| simple | painless | elementary | effortless | uncomplicated | straightforward |

# ADVENTUROUS ALTERNATIVES

| Grasshopper | Shinobi | Warrior | Samurai | Assassin | Grand Master |
|---|---|---|---|---|---|
| sweet | thrilling | impressive | remarkable | insane | unforgettable |
| eager | enthusiastic | roused | perky | ecstatic | aroused |
| dive | drop | tumble | descend | plummet | nosedive |
| well known | popular | leading | eminent | infamous | legendary |
| quick | speedy | rapid | nimble | blistering | breakneck |
| chubby | solid | overweight | plump | stout | rotund |
| spot | locate | notice | discover | acquire | pinpoint |
| flutter | hover | hang | float | glide | soar |
| fearful | alarmed | panicked | startled | spooked | petrified |
| pleasing | amusing | lively | entertaining | exciting | enthralling |
| collect | buy | gather | gain | obtain | acquire |
| vast | sizeable | tremendous | colossal | whopping | monumental |
| move | travel | visit | leave | continue | proceed |
| super | excellent | marvellous | exceptional | splendid | stupendous |
| lime | emerald | fern | moss | seaweed | pistachio |
| glad | delighted | thrilled | overjoyed | ecstatic | joyous |
| fear | dislike | loathe | detest | despise | abhor |
| keep | own | possess | boast | occupy | retain |
| support | aid | assist | guide | advise | contribute |
| stow | conceal | obstruct | shroud | camouflage | cache |
| hot | scorching | summery | blistering | roasting | tropical |

Vocabulary Ninja © Andrew Jennings, 2024

# ADVENTUROUS ALTERNATIVES

| Grasshopper | Shinobi | Warrior | Samurai | Assassin | Grand Master |
|---|---|---|---|---|---|
| injure | damage | wound | incapacitate | maim | mutilate |
| gripping | compelling | fascinating | absorbing | captivating | spellbinding |
| jolly | cheerful | cheery | bubbly | effervescent | exuberant |
| leap | spring | hop | bound | bounce | gambol |
| slay | destroy | eliminate | decimate | massacre | exterminate |
| idle | work-shy | sluggish | slothful | inactive | lethargic |
| twin | alike | similar | related | equivalent | akin |
| small | teeny | tiny | minor | compact | delicate |
| glance | stare | gape | peer | inspect | examine |
| booming | thunderous | deafening | blasting | raucous | ear-piercing |
| prize | worship | cherish | idolise | treasure | adore |
| beautiful | attractive | appealing | magical | adorable | exquisite |
| cause | create | produce | concoct | assemble | fabricate |
| huge | enormous | vast | monstrous | towering | Herculean |
| carry | transport | transfer | shift | switch | relocate |
| crept | lurked | ambled | shuffled | dashed | manoeuvred |
| funny | strange | puzzling | curious | baffling | inexplicable |
| unused | fresh | pristine | current | modern | contemporary |
| enjoyable | lovely | thoughtful | likeable | admirable | congenial |
| elderly | ancient | mature | historic | tattered | frayed |
| carrot | tiger | fire | honey | marmalade | tangerine |

# ADVENTUROUS ALTERNATIVES

| Grasshopper | Shinobi | Warrior | Samurai | Assassin | Grand Master |
|---|---|---|---|---|---|
| strawberry | rouge | rose | fuchsia | salmon | watermelon |
| interact | compete | frolic | cavort | engage | romp |
| charming | appealing | delightful | lovely | stunning | glamorous |
| plum | grape | jam | wine | violet | lavender |
| place | set | lay | deposit | position | plonk |
| swiftly | rapidly | speedily | briskly | hotfoot | lickety-split |
| calming | still | restful | soundless | serene | tranquil |
| actually | truly | genuinely | undoubtedly | certainly | unquestionably |
| cherry | scarlet | candy | blood | berry | crimson |
| rush | dash | scurry | scamper | hurtle | scuttle |
| unhappy | depressed | down | glum | blue | desolate |
| laughed | reported | stammered | thundered | insisted | acknowledged |
| afraid | fearful | nervous | panicky | alarmed | agitated |
| frightening | hair-raising | spine-chilling | daunting | formidable | blood-curdling |
| yell | cry | call | howl | bellow | shriek |
| nap | doze | rest | drowse | catnap | siesta |
| little | tiny | mini | minute | bijou | microscopic |
| suspend | cease | end | finish | conclude | terminate |
| mighty | meaty | powerful | robust | muscular | strapping |
| items | objects | property | gear | goods | possessions |

# ADVENTUROUS ALTERNATIVES

| Grasshopper | Shinobi | Warrior | Samurai | Assassin | Grand Master |
|---|---|---|---|---|---|
| foolish | ignorant | mindless | idiotic | moronic | brainless |
| immediately | instantly | promptly | abruptly | swiftly | instantaneously |
| remove | steal | seize | grab | capture | pilfer |
| chat | gossip | blabber | speak | converse | natter |
| inform | notify | alert | warn | advise | declare |
| awful | dreadful | appalling | revolting | atrocious | sickening |
| next | afterwards | soon after | later | instantly | subsequently |
| muse | ponder | reflect | deliberate | meditate | ruminate |
| reasoned | pondered | considered | mused | deliberated | contemplated |
| plain | unsightly | deformed | hideous | menacing | grotesque |
| miserable | down | dispirited | despondent | tearful | forlorn |
| hugely | overly | mightily | exceedingly | immensely | desperately |
| stroll | saunter | amble | plod | wander | roam |
| feeble | frail | flimsy | powerless | fragile | delicate |
| uncanny | eerie | bizarre | unconventional | peculiar | surreal |
| moved | proceeded | progressed | journeyed | departed | travelled |
| snow | pearl | ivory | bone | powder | porcelain |
| gold | corn | banana | lemon | mustard | butterscotch |
| babyish | youthful | adolescent | childlike | immature | juvenile |

# VOCABULARY LABORATORY

**The Vocabulary laboratory allows pupils to explore a word via a range of tasks and challenges. It is very straightforward to use.**

Vocabulary Ninja has developed a passion for the science of words after spending a great deal of time with my close friend, Dr Heinrich Frankenstein. Just as Dr Frankenstein studied chemical processes and the decay of living beings to gain an insight into the creation of life, so Vocabulary Ninja is fascinated with the anatomical breakdown of words and insights into the creation of language and life! *Evil laugh ensues*

The Vocabulary laboratory is a versatile resource designed to allow pupils to dive deep into the inner workings of a single word. One of the most impressive aspects of the Vocabulary laboratory is the incidental spelling, punctuation and grammar learning that can be gleaned from the accurate dissection of a word.

An interesting thing about the Vocabulary laboratory is that you will begin to get an amazing perspective into your pupils' lives – a great way to get to know them and personalise learning! Why? Well, because in the first instance, your pupils will apply the word to their own personal experiences. This reinforces my earlier comments about pupils' limited vocabulary pools being directly linked to their experiences of life. When you first start to use the Vocabulary laboratory resource and children have to apply the new word in their own context, I can nearly guarantee you will hear a significant number of sentences linked to

'my dog', 'my mum', 'my dad', 'my nana', and so on. It actually becomes amusing how many words can be accurately and humorously applied to 'my dad', 'my dog', 'my mum', 'my house', and so on. These are all people and places that your children are very familiar with, especially your less frequent readers. This is because some pupils will have very few 'varied and rich' experiences from their home life to apply the new language to. In this context, whole-class texts are a great way of providing a shared experience within your classroom, which all children can use and apply a word to.

The Vocabulary laboratory is a simple, yet highly effective resource that can be used with learners of all ages. The following pages provide an annotated Vocabulary laboratory for reference, a complex blank version of the resource for photocopying and a simpler version for younger learners.

## ESSENTIAL KNOWLEDGE

On the next page you will find the annotated example of the Vocabulary laboratory with the essential terminology you will need. Along with the basics, you should also make sure you are secure in your understanding of morphology – how words are put together.

**Target word** – Add the word that you want to focus on. This could be taken from the Word of the Day, a book or a conversation.

**Word class** – Word class can offer up some scintillating discussions, especially when the modifications to the word change the word class. By discussing all the subtleties and demonstrating them, we can create stronger links to the rest of the curriculum.

**Break it down** – Morphology is the study of the structure of words, essentially what the Vocabulary laboratory is all about. In this section, we want pupils to think about the target word on a morphological level – how the word is made up. Quite often, this will link nicely to the syllables a word contains but not always. Being aware of a word's syllable count is also a fantastic strategy for spelling. The word 'convention', for example, can be broken down into a prefix, root and suffix (con-vent-ion) and it has three syllables. This section of the Vocabulary laboratory may need more time being taught and discussed with the whole class to ensure understanding.

**Define it** – This is where you can embed the use of dictionary skills and locate an accurate definition of the target word. These skills are essential.

**Synonyms and antonyms** – Synonyms are words that have the same meaning as the target word. The Vocabulary laboratory gives pupils the chance to discuss and record words that have the same meaning. Antonyms are words that have the opposite meaning and can also be recorded in the Vocabulary laboratory. Often, a pupil's limited vocabulary can have a far-reaching impact on their communication skills and writing outcomes in education. Having regular opportunities to discuss synonyms and antonyms is important.

**Use in a sentence** – It is crucial that pupils have the opportunity to experiment and apply their understanding of a target word. This section provides a safe space for pupils to create sentences, edit and refine their ideas. This is also a fabulous opportunity to challenge pupils. Can they use a certain writing feature, such as a relative clause, thus embedding a range of other writing conventions? Drawing a picture adds to the aesthetic value of the learning, but also acts as a powerful tool for memorisation.

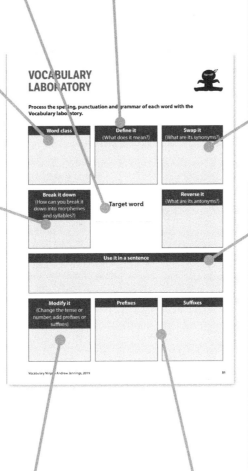

**Modify it** – Modifications are generally where the root of the word remains constant with various prefixes and suffixes being added to modify the word and its meaning. Depending on the target word you choose, a variety of different prefixes and suffixes will be available for pupils to modify the word meaning and the associated word class. The spelling, punctuation and grammar links here are endless. Spelling rules and strategies, tenses, plurals and rhymes can go here too.

**Prefixes and suffixes** – An understanding of how prefixes are attached to the beginning of words and suffixes to the end, and how they modify the meaning of the word, are essential skills for pupils to master. Regular use of the Vocabulary laboratory resource will expose pupils to a broad range of prefixes.

# VOCABULARY LABORATORY

**Process the spelling, punctuation and grammar of each word with the Vocabulary laboratory.**

| Word class | Define it (What does it mean?) | Swap it (What are its synonyms?) |
|---|---|---|

| Break it down (How can you break it down into morphemes and syllables?) | Target word _____ | Reverse it (What are its antonyms?) |
|---|---|---|

| Use it in a sentence |
|---|

| Modify it (Change the tense or number, add prefixes or suffixes) | Prefixes | Suffixes |
|---|---|---|

# VOCABULARY LABORATORY

**Process the spelling, punctuation and grammar of each word with the Vocabulary laboratory.**

## Target word

_____

| Define it |
|---|
|  |

| Use it in a sentence |
|---|
|  |

| Draw it |
|---|
|  |

# NOUN VS VERB

This is a classic Vocabulary Ninja resource, and one that I am very proud of. Noun vs verb drills down into pupils' understanding of word class in context. Depending on the sentence, a word could be taking on the role of a noun or a verb. Pupils will need to decide which side they are on when it comes to Noun vs verb.

## ESSENTIAL KNOWLEDGE

### Nouns

Pupils must understand what a noun is and the role it plays within a sentence. A noun is a word class that names something. Nouns name places, people, objects, emotions, thoughts, and so on. They can also be broken down into subcategories, e.g. proper nouns, common nouns and abstract nouns.

### Verbs

Verbs are often known as 'doing words'. This phrase unfortunately doesn't help pupils to fully grasp what a verb is and the role it has in a sentence. Verbs show the states of being, doing and having; *be, do* and *have* are all verbs. Being able to identify the subject or object within a sentence can also help to identify the verb.

## Understanding words within the sentence context

Pupils must understand that certain words, for example, the word *walk*, can act as a noun or a verb, depending on the sentence. For instance, if you were to 'go for a walk', *walk* in this context would be a noun. Whereas, if you were to 'walk along the street', *walk* would be a verb. Sometimes the word or phrase that precedes the target word (in this instance 'walk'), can help us decide whether it is a noun or verb. If the word is preceded by an article or determiner, e.g. a walk or the walk, this helps us to know that the target word is a noun. A verb will often be preceded by the word *to*, an auxiliary verb or even a pronoun, e.g. 'I walk', 'we walk'.

> Images or small video clips, or drama exercises, are great for illustrating the difference between a noun and a verb to pupils. Give them the same word in two different sentences and ask them to act it out. How does the target word function?

# NOUN VS VERB

**Decide if the target word is being used as a noun or a verb.**

| Target word | Context | Word class |
|---|---|---|
| crush | There was a crush in the corridor before playtime. | |
| bottle | We needed to bottle as much water as possible. | |
| paint | Everyone used the paint with care and attention. | |
| watch | His watch had stopped working. | |
| block | He raised his hand to block the sunlight. | |
| arm | They need to arm themselves before the battle begins. | |
| picture | He couldn't picture everybody playing nicely together. | |
| level | Jimmy used the spade to level off the ground. | |
| clap | Mr Rogers could hear a clap, but wasn't sure where. | |
| peel | Next to the bin, there was lots of fruit peel on the floor. | |
| spoon | Helen was asked to spoon the sand into the tray. | |
| fire | There was a huge fire which could be seen for miles. | |
| light | As it was bedtime, Alex needed to switch off his light. | |
| dip | Peter wanted to dip his biscuit into the warm tea. | |
| cover | The book cover was tatty and frayed at the edges. | |
| book | Mum needed to book the tickets before they left. | |
| train | We need to train harder if we are to win the competition. | |
| frown | My frown just couldn't be turned upside down. | |

# SPaG FACTS AND SPaG SPOTTER

The SPaG facts exercise outlines some of the basic terminology that we want all pupils to be able to identify and understand.

SPaG facts are the building blocks of spelling, punctuation and grammar. Pupils will need to be able to carry out simple tasks that require them to understand some of the most basic aspects of SPaG, such as identifying word classes, using the correct determiners, adding punctuation and much more. SPaG spotter explores a whole host of spelling, punctuation and grammar issues. 'So what do the pupils have to do?' I hear you ask. They have to spot the SPaG! Simple, but super effective. Children will need to spot the indicated SPaG elements within each sentence. It's great practice and great fun.

## ESSENTIAL KNOWLEDGE

SPaG facts and SPaG spotter are comprehensive tools for investigating word classes and grammar in sentences.

### Pronouns

*I, he she, we, they, those, her, his*

Pronouns can replace nouns, help to build cohesion and avoid repetition.

### Determiners

*a, an, the, this, that, those, these, a few, many,* numbers and pronouns

Determiners do what they say: they help us determine noun groups, tense, quantity and possession.

### Articles

*a, an, the*

Articles are used to refer to nouns; there are three of them in English.

### Modal verbs

*will, might, could, won't, can't, may, can, must*

Modal verbs help suggest degrees of possibility, from impossible to certainty.

### Nouns

Refer to the Noun vs verb resource (page 86) for more information.

### Adjectives

Commonly known as 'describing words' in the classroom, but calling adjectives describing words doesn't help pupils to fully understand their purpose. Adjectives have a close relationship with nouns – they help to add information and detail about the noun. Adjectives often come before nouns.

### Verbs

Refer to the Noun vs verb (page 86) resource for more information.

### Adverbs

Adverbs can offer increasing levels of detail to a verb by 'adding' information to the 'verb', thus the term 'adverb'.

### Prepositions

*on, in, over, under, next to, below, before, after, inside, through*

Prepositions tell us more information about an object's location in place or time. A great way of remembering what a preposition tells us about is to spot the word 'position' in 'preposition'.

## CONJUNCTIONS

There are two types of conjunction: coordinating conjunctions and subordinating conjunctions.

*for, and, nor, but, or, yet, so*

Coordinating conjunctions are used to join two independent clauses. The coordinating conjunction defines the relationship between the two clauses.

*although, when, because, meanwhile, however* (not exhaustive)

Subordinating conjunctions normally introduce a subordinate clause. The subordinate clause needs to be used in conjunction with an independent clause in order to act as a coherent sentence.

> Don't use SPaG cliché phrases. Be precise with your feedback and give examples of SPaG in context.

# SPaG FACTS

## Give examples of these types of word.

| | | | |
|---|---|---|---|
| noun | | possessive pronoun | |
| verb | | subordinating conjunction | |
| adjective | | coordinating conjunction | |
| adverb | | proper noun | |
| pronoun | | collective noun | |
| article | | abstract noun | |
| determiner | | concrete noun | |
| preposition | | quantifier | |

## Rewrite these words in their expanded form.

| | |
|---|---|
| can't | |
| isn't | |
| won't | |
| couldn't | |
| mustn't | |
| didn't | |
| I'll | |

## Rewrite these words in the past tense.

| | |
|---|---|
| kick | |
| move | |
| catch | |
| remain | |
| fight | |
| perform | |
| blow | |

## Circle apostrophes for possession.

| | |
|---|---|
| Jenny's car | We mustn't |
| I'll be late | Mark's dinner |
| The man's hat | Don't |

## Circle the modal verbs.

| | |
|---|---|
| would | might |
| fill | park |
| should | may |

# SPaG FACTS

## Give examples of these types of word.

| | |
|---|---|
| noun | |
| verb | |
| adjective | |
| adverb | |
| pronoun | |
| article | |
| determiner | |
| preposition | |

| | |
|---|---|
| possessive pronoun | |
| subordinating conjunction | |
| coordinating conjunction | |
| proper noun | |
| collective noun | |
| abstract noun | |
| concrete noun | |
| quantifier | |

## Add punctuation accurately.

| | |
|---|---|
| , | Under the table the slimy frog jumped onto my foot. |
| . | I love ice cream |
| ? | Who is it |
| ! | What a day |
| ( ) | Mr Dot the teacher was eating his lunch. |
| " " | Get lost, boomed the man. |
| ; | We couldn't be beaten it just couldn't happen. |

## Add an appropriate prefix.

| | |
|---|---|
| | believe |
| | freeze |
| | plane |
| | paid |
| | charge |
| | fill |
| | usual |

## Add the capital letters, commas and full stops.

yesterday we went for lunch with mr johnson jenny and phillip

## Circle subordinating conjunctions.

| | |
|---|---|
| until | whether |
| regret | fool |
| although | since |

# SPaG SPOTTER

## Circle the relevant part of speech.

| Can you spot...? | Context |
| --- | --- |
| the nouns | The boys were playing football in the park with their friends. |
| the verbs | Clean up your room and help your sister with her homework. |
| the adjectives | The crumbling mountain couldn't support the delicate ecosystem. |
| the adverbs | Singing loudly, I was completely relaxed. |
| the articles | I would love to have a friend like you. |
| the determiner | If only I could find those comfortable slippers. |
| the prepositions | Jamal was perched on the table while Alex hid under the table. |
| a coordinating conjunction | We were all ready to leave, but Fred had forgotten his bag. |
| the pronouns | She was so cool; I admired her so much. |
| a subordinating conjunction | Although it was late, Paul wanted to stay up to watch the film. |
| a noun phrase | I could see lots of yummy, cold yoghurt. |

## Edit the sentence to make it correct.

| Can you add...? | Context |
| --- | --- |
| a comma to make a fronted adverbial | Even though she was tall I knew I could still beat her. |
| commas in the list | Even Derek Gina Kazuki and Mark were going to the party. |
| a / an | The class dearly wanted to adopt _____ elephant. |
| brackets | Mr Hill the class teacher was determined to beat the children. |
| the capital letters | underneath the manchester skyline, jenny could see mary crying. |

# PICTURE PROCESSOR

The Picture processor processes and decodes an image into the SPaG that it is made up of. It is a fantastic visual resource and is provided with stimulus images so you can use it straightaway. The Picture processor is underpinned by the power of three: in each section, the pupil is only allowed to add three items. In the case of this resource, less is more! Pupils have to finish off by pulling all of the processed words back together in the form of a detailed sentence.

**Nouns** – When you look at the image, whatever you can see is a noun!

**Pronouns and noun phrases** – Noun phrases are groups of words that revolve around a head word, the noun or possibly an indefinite pronoun.

**Fronted adverbials** – Fronted adverbials are groups of words that help to begin sentences in a more varied fashion. They tell us more about how, where, when, what, who and why. They can help to add more detail to the sentence. A good way to create them is to look at the image, think about where the image is, what is happening, and what time of day it is.

**Adjectives** – The building blocks of any great sentence! Once adjectives have been mastered, ensure that pupils understand expanded noun phrases, so they can create them and identify them in other sentences. When you look at the image, how would you describe what you see?

**Verbs** – Pupils will need to think carefully about the tense they use in regards to the image they see. What is it that the subject or objects are being, doing or having?

**Prepositions** – Prepositions add even more detail to a sentence and can go unnoticed. For additional challenge, pupils should be shown how to create and identify prepositional phrases.

**Adverbs** – Adverbs can help the reader to understand in greater detail *how* something is occurring. Often, adverbs end in -ly, but not always! They are superb for bringing a sentence to life.

**Sentence** – The final task is to create a detailed sentence using some or all of the grammatical strands. To use them all, pupils will also need to be skilled at using commas and other punctuation to create multi-clause sentences.

**Conjunctions** – In the finished sentence, we will most likely only see one conjunction as not all conjunctions will suit the image. More able pupils should be thinking about subordinating conjunctions, rather than coordinating ones.

**Determiners** – Determiners help us to determine noun groups, tense, quantity and possession.

Vocabulary Ninja © Andrew Jennings, 2024

# PICTURE PROCESSOR

Look at this photograph for one minute. Discuss what you see with a partner, then make a list all of the words you have used to describe the photograph.

Use the power of three. You can only add three items to each box.

| Nouns: | Adjectives: | Verbs: |
|---|---|---|
| | | |
| **Pronouns and noun phrases:** | **Prepositions:** | **Adverbs:** |
| | | |
| **Fronted adverbials:** | **Conjunctions:** | **Determiners:** |
| | | |

**Sentence:**

# PICTURE PROCESSOR

Look at this photograph for one minute. Discuss what you see with a partner, then make a list all of the words you have used to describe the photograph.

**NINJA NOTES**

Use the power of three. You can only add three items to each box.

| Nouns: | Adjectives: | Verbs: |
|---|---|---|
| | | |
| **Pronouns and noun phrases:** | **Prepositions:** | **Adverbs:** |
| | | |
| **Fronted adverbials:** | **Conjunctions:** | **Determiners:** |
| | | |

**Sentence:**

_____

_____

_____

# VOCABULARY VAULT

In this chapter, you'll find vocabulary for close to 60 different topic areas linked to the National Curriculum. Vocabulary Ninja has identified significant figures, adjectives, verbs and nouns that will all support the writing process. An estimate of words in this section is approximately 50 different words per topic over 50 topics – that's 2,000 different pieces of vocabulary ready for staff and pupils to use instantly!

# VOCABULARY VAULT

## Anglo-Saxons

| Battle of Hastings | William the Conqueror | Nouns | Adjectives | Verbs |
|---|---|---|---|---|
| 1066 | Norman | Angle | resourceful | farm |
| arrow | Normandy | Saxon | versatile | scavenge |
| eye | superior | Jute | practical | weave |
| exhaustion | well-trained | Beowulf | adept | worship |
| conquered | crowned | farmer | creative | craft |
| France | invader | Sutton Hoo | violent | trade |
| Norway | castles | tapestry | aggressive | battle |
| Sussex | victorious | weaponry | skilled | attack |
| Senlac Hill | king | ship | bold | voyage |
| cavalry | famous | Mercia | marauding | entertain |

## Animals

| Animals | Animals | Nouns | Adjectives | Verbs |
|---|---|---|---|---|
| elephant | wolf | horn | furry | whimper |
| giraffe | badger | paw | colourful | snarl |
| lion | meerkat | tusk | dangerous | swallow |
| rhinoceros | tortoise | snout | slithery | nibble |
| kangaroo | woodpecker | tentacle | stealthy | charge |
| orangutan | vulture | hump | camouflaged | crawl |
| whale | flamingo | antler | elegant | creep |
| octopus | kingfisher | flipper | poisonous | swoop |
| hippopotamus | shark | feather | strong | pounce |
| swordfish | jellyfish | venom | feathered | gnaw |

# VOCABULARY VAULT

## Anne Frank

| Anne | Camps | Nouns | Adjectives | Verbs |
|------|-------|-------|------------|-------|
| diary | concentration | sister | brave | invade |
| Jewish | Auschwitz | parent | anxious | forbid |
| persecuted | prison | World War | hidden | arrest |
| imprisoned | labour | religion | intelligent | evacuate |
| Bergen-Belsen | death | Jew | tragic | publish |
| secret annexe | torture | Margo | abhorrent | survive |
| arrested | conditions | Adolf Hitler | descriptive | liberate |
| Amsterdam | Holocaust | Kitty | worried | evade |
| Otto / Edith | millions | annex | fearful | defy |
| bookcase | deceit | Nazi | courageous | grieve |

## Capital cities

| Cities | Cities | Nouns | Adjectives | Verbs |
|--------|--------|-------|------------|-------|
| London | Cairo | museum | ancient | discover |
| Edinburgh | Tunis | art galleries | historic | explore |
| Cardiff | Kabul | river | beautiful | travel |
| Dublin | Bangkok | war | famous | build |
| Madrid | Seoul | culture | imperial | photograph |
| Rome | Bucharest | palace | metropolitan | speak |
| Paris | Beijing | landmark | vast | describe |
| Oslo | Brasilia | government | crowded | learn |
| Helsinki | Lima | tourism | flourishing | immerse |
| Zagreb | Buenos Aires | cathedral | thriving | create |

# VOCABULARY VAULT

## Christopher Columbus

| Columbus | Explorer | Nouns | Adjectives | Verbs |
|---|---|---|---|---|
| navigator | discover | King Ferdinand | adventurous | sail |
| explorer | find | sailor | bold | convince |
| sailor | search | voyager | rebellious | explore |
| Italian | explore | New World | innovative | settle |
| voyages | navigate | spices | naive | return |
| Americas | sail | gold | personable | build |
| East Indies | voyage | Spain | intelligent | capture |
| Indians | sickness | disease | famous | rescue |
| colonise | death | Santa Maria | dangerous | starve |
| exploit | indigenous | compass | historic | enslave |

## Climate zones

| Polar | Temperate | Tropical | Desert | Weather |
|---|---|---|---|---|
| freezing | moderate | equator | no rainfall | blizzard |
| icy | four seasons | wet | Sahara | storm |
| snow | variable | monsoon | dry conditions | torrential |
| below zero | spring | rain forest | cactus | drought |
| Siberia | summer | predictable | hibernate | flood |
| poles | winter | floods | sand | temperature |
| inhospitable | inhabited | mud slides | heat | rainbow |
| Arctic | unpredictable | drought | cold | downpour |
| Antarctica | Europe | humid | camel | drizzle |
| penguin | London | insects | lizards | thermometer |

 Vocabulary Ninja © Andrew Jennings, 2024

# VOCABULARY VAULT

## Dinosaurs

| T-Rex | Pterodactyl | Nouns | Adjectives | Verbs |
|---|---|---|---|---|
| lizard | pterosaur | extinction | deadly | discover |
| theropod | reptile | dinosaur | sluggish | scavenge |
| Cretaceous | carnivore | predator | agile | bite |
| tyrant | fish | carnivore | swift | roam |
| muscular | wings | food chain | primitive | stomp |
| aggressive | muscle / skin | herbivore | fearsome | evolve |
| predator | fingers | scales | magnificent | fly |
| short arms | unique | camouflage | beastly | hunt |
| scavenger | jagged beak | museum | colourful | forage |
| intelligent | recognisable | meteor | enormous | roar |

## Egyptians

| Tutankhamun | H. Carter | Nouns | Adjectives | Verbs |
|---|---|---|---|---|
| boy-king | famous | mummy | mighty | mummify |
| malaria | explorer | hieroglyph | knowledgeable | entomb |
| entombed | archaeologist | cartouche | democratic | poison |
| frail | Egyptologist | River Nile | civilised | unearth |
| King Tut | excavated | pyramid | decadent | immortalise |
| excavated | wealthy | Giza | wealthy | embalm |
| deformed | artist | Sphinx | scientific | betray |
| mysterious | lymphoma | canopic jar | primitive | bribe |
| pharaoh | treasures | inscription | prosperous | invent |
| sarcophagus | historic | desert | intelligent | bicker |

# VOCABULARY VAULT

## Electricity

| Appliances | Key Words | Nouns | Adjectives | Verbs |
|---|---|---|---|---|
| iron | conductor | energy | tidal | open |
| television | insulator | turbine | solar | close |
| socket | open | power station | clean | surge |
| tablet | closed | motor | dirty | bridge |
| mobile phone | circuit | fossil fuel | cheap | observe |
| lamp | incomplete | current | renewable | resist |
| toaster | broken | voltage | nuclear | brighten |
| microwave | flow | battery | geothermal | light |
| hairdryer | resistance | pylon | dangerous | burn |
| speaker | static | ammeter | safe | investigate |

## Explorers

| Captain Cook | Francis Drake | Nouns | Adjectives | Verbs |
|---|---|---|---|---|
| British | circumnavigate | pathfinder | illustrious | navigate |
| cartographer | Spanish | captain | audacious | transport |
| navigator | Armada | conditions | intrepid | explore |
| South Pacific | Atlantic | weather | resolute | discover |
| apprentice | New World | weapon | infamous | exchange |
| Royal Navy | victorious | route | adventurous | research |
| Endeavour | revenge | expedition | ardent | battle |
| healthy crew | pirate | merchant | curious | inspire |
| Whitby | privateer | trailblazer | wealthy | trade |
| Easter Island | The Dragon | ration | vast | traverse |

# VOCABULARY VAULT

## Fairy tales

| Red Riding Hood | Goldilocks | Nouns | Adjectives | Verbs |
|---|---|---|---|---|
| wolf | careless | princess | cruel | trick |
| help | chair | castle | deadly | touch |
| Grandma | porridge | bed | wooden | protect |
| cottage | three bears | forest | beautiful | believe |
| basket | sleepy | wolf | magical | befriend |
| cloak | beautiful | chair | loveable | climb |
| woodcutter | frustrated | kitchen | deformed | discard |
| devour | kitchen | axe | enchanted | smell |
| disguise | breakfast | cow | dangerous | disguise |
| rescue | wandered | harp | sneaky | chase |

## Famous women

| Rosa Parks | Malala Yousafzai | Nouns | Adjectives | Verbs |
|---|---|---|---|---|
| activist | human rights | respect | heroic | enthuse |
| bus | Pakistan | legend | brave | stand |
| boycott | education | hardship | plucky | demonstrate |
| segregation | Islam | challenge | radical | protest |
| different | multilingual | story | enlightened | convince |
| NAACP | Taliban | pioneer | unwavering | defy |
| arrested | women | equality | unsung | accomplish |
| appeal | shot | adversity | valiant | survive |
| symbol | survivor | integrity | veracious | struggle |
| freedom | Nobel Peace | resilience | honest | persist |

# VOCABULARY VAULT

## Florence Nightingale

| Florence | Life and Work | Nouns | Adjectives | Verbs |
|---|---|---|---|---|
| nurse | training | heroine | kind | nurse |
| nursing | wounded | Russia | heroic | wash |
| Crimean War | diseases | Lady with the Lamp | thoughtful | clean |
| soldiers | death | patient | caring | challenge |
| famous | sickness | Scutari | courageous | revolutionise |
| hospital | injuries | Miss Smith | inspirational | impose |
| Crimea | cleaning | Florence | ambitious | train |
| Sidney Herbert | cleanliness | anaesthetic | loving | love |
| doctors | patients | museum | devoted | save |
| medicine | investigate | founded | selfless | rescue |

## Great Fire of London

| London | Samuel Pepys | Nouns | Adjectives | Verbs |
|---|---|---|---|---|
| Thames | diary | Great Fire | raging | decimate |
| capital | British | bakery | smoky | demolish |
| medieval | government | houses | burning | smoke |
| narrow | Royal Navy | timber | consuming | extinguish |
| sanitation | Star Inn | gunpowder | damaging | damage |
| unhygienic | primary source | plague | blistering | spread |
| Pudding Lane | writing | drought | infernal | engulf |
| combustible | record | devastation | vicious | explode |
| population | first person | September | consuming | douse |
| common | detail | flame | hellish | record |

Vocabulary Ninja © Andrew Jennings, 2024

# VOCABULARY VAULT

## Greeks

| Zeus | Spartan | Nouns | Adjectives | Verbs |
|---|---|---|---|---|
| imposing | fitness | Hades | civilised | invade |
| immortal | military | Sparta | primitive | conquer |
| thunder | fearless | Zeus | united | honour |
| lightning | discipline | Hera | aristocratic | drape |
| titans | toughness | Xerxes | provocative | battle |
| Olympus | phalanx | Paris | ancient | preside |
| Hera | excellence | Archimedes | religious | defeat |
| mortals | Leonidas | Parthenon | cultural | sacrifice |
| revered | exercise | Mount Olympus | ruthless | encounter |
| merciful | rigorous | Aphrodite | artistic | crush |

## Gunpowder Plot

| Guy Fawkes | Robert Catesby | Nouns | Adjectives | Verbs |
|---|---|---|---|---|
| gunpowder | leader | revenge | devious | survive |
| guarding | mastermind | battle | bloody | attempt |
| discovered | recruiter | conspirator | murderous | thwart |
| arrested | Catholic | Parliament | horrific | assassinate |
| explosives | assassinate | London | repulsive | ignite |
| beneath | revolt | bonfire | organised | destroy |
| tortured | influential | November 5th | sneaky | conspire |
| patsy | shot | guard | illegal | prevent |
| cellars | letter | treason | tactical | hang |
| effigy | fled | barrel | infamous | murder |

# VOCABULARY VAULT

## Habitats

| Burrow | Nest | Dam | Polar | Adjectives |
|--------|------|-----|-------|------------|
| hole | birds | water | North Pole | vast |
| tunnel | laying eggs | barrier | South Pole | narrow |
| dig | safety | restrict | penguin | underground |
| hollow | height | flow | cold | damp |
| set | roost | stream | windy | fragile |
| den | shelter | reservoir | snow | solid |
| dwelling | construct | flood | tundra | murky |
| safety | hatching | river | polar bear | secure |
| retreat | twigs | floodgates | Arctic | snug |
| earth | storage | irrigation | Antarctic | wild |

## Holocaust

| Hitler | Heydrich | Nouns | Adjectives | Verbs |
|--------|----------|-------|------------|-------|
| Auschwitz | high-ranking | antisemitism | bloody | execute |
| cruel | chief lieutenant | Bergen-Belsen | ghastly | transport |
| criminal | the SS | death squads | callous | slaughter |
| holocaust | architect | Gestapo | unforgivable | cleanse |
| Führer | deportation | gas chamber | wretched | escape |
| embroiled | authorised | Nazi | infamous | exterminate |
| invader | retribution | genocide | noxious | symbolise |
| vain | Himmler | children | calculated | murder |
| dictator | murderer | women | cruel | imprison |
| racist | ruthless | Mein Kampf | nightmarish | deport |

# VOCABULARY VAULT

## Human body

| Skeleton | Organs | Nouns | Adjectives | Verbs |
|---|---|---|---|---|
| cranium | brain | nerves | muscular | regulate |
| mandible | heart | cell | physical | break down |
| sternum | lungs | carbon dioxide | obese | produce |
| femur | kidney | oxygen | magnificent | eat |
| fibula | liver | muscle | fragile | digest |
| tibia | intestine | bones | tall | remove |
| radius | bowel | pulse | rigid | transport |
| ulna | skin | ligament | breakable | circulate |
| patella | blood vessels | artery | vital | absorb |
| humerus | spinal cord | vein | overweight | breathe |

## Knights and castles

| Knights | Castles | Nouns | Adjectives | Verbs |
|---|---|---|---|---|
| sword | stone | tower | metallic | applaud |
| shield | moat | chainmail | deadly | pillage |
| brave | defence | dragon | shimmering | destroy |
| loyal | protect | tournament | loyal | canter |
| well-trained | villagers | castle | dangerous | prevail |
| protector | drawbridge | helmet | wooden | honour |
| honour | gatehouse | squire | impassable | barrage |
| military | dungeon | gauntlet | heavy | fire |
| armour | courtyard | catapult | powerful | launch |
| horse | ramparts | jester | tough | provoke |

# VOCABULARY VAULT

## Light

| Isaac Newton | Eratosthenes | Nouns | Adjectives | Verbs |
|---|---|---|---|---|
| scientist | Alexandria | metal | colourful | measure |
| prism | library | wood | dark | appear |
| wave | geometry | battery | light | illuminate |
| spectrum | sciences | mirror | short | bounce |
| theory | Syene | source | long | reflect |
| particle | discovery | sun | faint | permeate |
| experiment | world | glass | translucent | distort |
| prove | sticks | shadow | artificial | absorb |
| beam | paper | light | partial | erupt |
| refract | water well | rainbow | opaque | create |

## London

| Buildings | Places | Nouns | Adjectives | Verbs |
|---|---|---|---|---|
| Shard | River Thames | history | international | travel |
| London Eye | Hyde Park | culture | historic | visit |
| Buckingham | Covent Garden | airport | natural | guard |
| palace | Camden Lock | bicycle | bustling | experience |
| Wembley | West End | parks | eclectic | march |
| Downing Street | London Zoo | music | rich | purchase |
| Big Ben | Westminster | tourist | inventive | observe |
| O2 Arena | Notting Hill | underground | cultured | explore |
| St. Paul's | China Town | tube | traditional | cycle |
| cathedral | Greenwich | black cab | picturesque | ride |

 Vocabulary Ninja © Andrew Jennings, 2024

# VOCABULARY VAULT

## Mini-beasts

| Earthworm | Ant | Nouns | Adjectives | Verbs |
|---|---|---|---|---|
| soil | strong insect | ecosystem | slimy | hibernate |
| slither | six legs | environment | abundant | consume |
| no legs | team | habitat | powerful | shelter |
| tunnel | social | insect | slithering | transform |
| replicate | colony | wings | predatory | tunnel |
| sections | queen | exoskeleton | poisonous | pollinate |
| hermaphrodite | drone | mollusc | delicate | devour |
| moisture | forage | sting | smooth | scuttle |
| annelid | worker | grasshopper | rough | inject |
| decomposer | black / red | centipede | aggressive | crush |

## Mountains

| Edmund Hillary | Mt. Everest | Nouns | Adjectives | Verbs |
|---|---|---|---|---|
| explorer | mountain | mountaineer | magnificent | ascend |
| first | highest | climber | sheer | prevail |
| influential | 8,849 metres | piste | imposing | perish |
| inspiration | Holy Mother | disaster | volcanic | endure |
| Himalayas | K2 | Tenzing Norgay | inaccessible | climb |
| Khumbu Icefall | 290 deaths | ascent | impassable | cripple |
| beekeeper | blizzard | record | beautiful | mount |
| summit | avalanche | peak | picturesque | conquer |
| Sherpa | base camp | weather | snow-capped | emaciate |
| humble | climbing | equipment | royal | persist |

# VOCABULARY VAULT

## Natural disasters

| Tsunami | Earthquake | Nouns | Adjectives | Verbs |
|---|---|---|---|---|
| earthquake | tectonic | geologist | catastrophic | collapse |
| seismic | aftershock | ocean | volatile | barrage |
| location | fault | fault lines | unstable | destroy |
| tidal wave | amplitude | hurricanes | appalling | restore |
| ocean | core | tornado | phenomenal | evacuate |
| deadly | tremor | volcano | chaotic | warn |
| flood | mantle | flood | violent | surge |
| underwater | crust | mud slides | unforeseen | tremble |
| debris | magnitude | storm | imminent | devastate |
| coastal | Richter Scale | death | menacing | grieve |

## On a farm

| Animals | Vehicles | Nouns | Adjectives | Verbs |
|---|---|---|---|---|
| cow | tractor | farmer | muddy | open |
| horse | jeep | hatchery | smelly | close |
| sheep | car | vermin | disgusting | feed |
| sheep dog | van | fertiliser | loud | herd |
| bull | combine harvester | trough | noisy | gallop |
| pig | motorbike | stable | messy | shout |
| chicken | plough | manure | isolated | catch |
| cockerel | hay baler | paddock | difficult | milk |
| mouse | cultivator | farmhouse | fertile | sell |
| goose | quad bike | tractor | tiring | groom |

Vocabulary Ninja © Andrew Jennings, 2024

# VOCABULARY VAULT

## Pirates

| John Silver | Pirate Ship | Nouns | Adjectives | Verbs |
|---|---|---|---|---|
| cunning | plank | eye-patch | dirty | plan |
| villain | Jolly Roger | flag | ruthless | sail |
| parrot | wooden | palm tree | dangerous | attack |
| one-legged | crow's nest | treasure | strong | plunder |
| crutch | overboard | gold | swashbuckling | board |
| disability | barrel | cannon | fearsome | parlay |
| fearsome | galleon | sea | golden | fight |
| courageous | first mate | shipwreck | jagged | navigate |
| infamous | cutlass | chest | scruffy | steal |
| silver | anchor | mast | lazy | drink |

## Plague

| Doctors | Symptoms | Nouns | Adjectives | Verbs |
|---|---|---|---|---|
| demonic | buboes | sewage | epidemic | treat |
| spices | fever | fleas | rampant | endure |
| herbs | chills | plague | dreadful | transmit |
| overpower | pain | smoke | severe | infect |
| repel | vomiting | sanitation | profound | quarantine |
| evil | bleeding | exodus | unknown | destroy |
| protect | gangrene | London | infectious | kill |
| infection | blackening | swelling | contagious | prescribe |
| beak | headaches | remedy | chronic | imprison |
| rats | legions | streets | sudden | diagnose |

# VOCABULARY VAULT

## Plants

| Plants | Plants | Nouns | Adjectives | Verbs |
|---|---|---|---|---|
| flower | stigma | flower | scientific | unearth |
| leaf | style | garden | leafy | observe |
| stem | ovary | greenhouse | tolerant | protect |
| roots | sepal | seed | stunning | decompose |
| sun | stem | compost | green | water |
| water | filament | insect | fleshy | feed |
| grow | stamen | pollen | giant | aerate |
| seed | germinate | bucket | tolerant | create |
| weed | pollinate | tray | withered | bloom |
| leaves | photosynthesis | soil | fragrant | produce |

## Plastic pollution

| Plastic | Affected | Danger | Adjectives | Verbs |
|---|---|---|---|---|
| bottle | sea birds | hazard | microscopic | protect |
| micro-bead | fish | pollutant | durable | clean |
| carrier bag | algae | pollution | useful | save |
| food wrapping | humans | damaging | nuisance | remove |
| flip flops | whales | toxic | impossible | recycle |
| straws | dolphins | debris | unsustainable | consume |
| balloon | crabs | suffocate | disgusting | gather |
| netting | turtles | starvation | preventable | educate |
| tyres | sea life | garbage | widespread | ingest |
| tubs and trays | everyone | infested | polluted | swallow |

# VOCABULARY VAULT

## Potions

| Wizard | Witch | Nouns | Adjectives | Verbs |
|---|---|---|---|---|
| beastly | monstrous | mixture | toxic | inject |
| bearded | gruesome | antidote | lethal | enchant |
| powerful | repugnant | cork | magical | combine |
| wise | mythical | container | viscous | curse |
| insane | matted | vapour | enchanting | froth |
| wicked | feline | alchemist | powerful | blend |
| ancient | raspy | spell | secret | dissolve |
| legendary | serrated | sorcerer | poisonous | hex |
| evil | cackle | charm | harmful | invent |
| staff | mighty | elixir | unsafe | transform |

## Rainforest

| Orangutan | Tree Frog | Noun | Adjectives | Verbs |
|---|---|---|---|---|
| ape | amphibian | canopy | wondrous | cover |
| leaves | frog | layer | diverse | scavenge |
| insects | vibrant | habitat | mature | discover |
| mammal | sticky pads | reptiles | extensive | rain |
| bulky | foliage | mammals | remote | locate |
| solitary | insectivore | species | dangerous | evaporate |
| forager | rivers | oxygen | dense | reproduce |
| creative | ponds | nutrients | temperate | contain |
| intelligent | tadpole | plants | moist | adapt |
| endangered | vertebrate | eco-system | rotting | survive |

# VOCABULARY VAULT

## Religious festivals

| Ramadan | Diwali | Nouns | Adjectives | Verbs |
|---|---|---|---|---|
| Eid Al-Fitr | Hinduism | Islam | friendly | pray |
| fasting | festival | Muslim | colourful | share |
| Quran | light | Jesus | royal | eat |
| five pillars | lantern | Quran | historic | celebrate |
| sawm | Sikhism | Nian | welcoming | fast |
| zakat | Rama | tradition | inventive | illuminate |
| taraweeh | Sita | parade | traditional | forgive |
| salat | bindi | celebrate | loud | receive |
| prayer | diva lamp | prayer | noisy | gather |
| Islam | rangoli | decorations | crowded | help |

## Rivers

| Thames | Nile | Noun | Adjectives | Verbs |
|---|---|---|---|---|
| London | Africa | source | microscopic | travel |
| bridges | Egypt | erosion | durable | purify |
| islands | 6,695 km | tide | useful | meet |
| London Eye | 4,160 miles | sea | nuisance | engulf |
| 346 km | Mediterranean | dam | impossible | plunge |
| 215 miles | longest | current | unsustainable | collect |
| pollution | fertile | mudflats | disgusting | erode |
| salty | lakes | river bank | preventable | deposit |
| capital | papyrus | stream | widespread | fill |
| North Sea | flood plain | meander | polluted | rise |

Vocabulary Ninja © Andrew Jennings, 2024

# VOCABULARY VAULT

## Romans

| Caesar | Soldier | Nouns | Adjectives | Verbs |
|---|---|---|---|---|
| betrayed | well-trained | Rome | vicious | march |
| ruler | loyal | toga | ancient | rule |
| friend | fearless | empire | proud | plot |
| mastermind | skilled | slave | illustrious | execute |
| reckless | obedient | ballista | warlike | enslave |
| vain | iconic | chariot | wealthy | duel |
| ambitious | brutal | villa | infamous | betray |
| dictator | ruthless | gladiator | primitive | skirmish |
| visionary | legionary | amphitheatre | mighty | bicker |
| assassinated | centurion | standard | decadent | backstab |

## Seaside

| Wildlife | Beach | Noun | Adjectives | Verbs |
|---|---|---|---|---|
| seagull | sand | lifeguard | calm | paddle |
| crab | sandcastle | rock pool | glistening | relax |
| jellyfish | sun | dock | windswept | visit |
| fish | shell | boat | rocky | stroll |
| shrimp | bucket | shell | tropical | float |
| tadpole | space | donkey | golden | snack |
| starfish | hat | current | interesting | construct |
| mussels | dune | spade | calm | gallop |
| seal | pier | pebble | popular | play |
| puffin | shore | bucket | crowded | splash |

# VOCABULARY VAULT

## Seasons

| Spring | Summer | Autumn | Winter | Weather |
|--------|--------|--------|--------|---------|
| March | June | September | December | blizzard |
| April | July | October | January | temperature |
| May | August | November | February | wildlife |
| buds | sunflower | leaves | ice | flood |
| lamb | lawnmower | rain | snowflakes | drought |
| egg | holiday | brown | jumper | vegetation |
| chick | beach | orange | gloves | foliage |
| blossom | park | red | snowman | warmth |
| rain | paddling | harvest | woolly hat | growth |
| grow | storms | foliage | scarf | hibernate |

## Space

| Tim Peake | Neil Armstrong | Planets | Adjectives | Verbs |
|-----------|----------------|---------|------------|-------|
| pilot | Buzz Aldrin | Mercury | lunar | launch |
| expedition | astronaut | Venus | bold | orbit |
| military | engineer | Earth | regimented | land |
| European | Moon | Mars | distant | pilot |
| Space | American | Jupiter | perilous | breathe |
| Agency | lunar module | Saturn | unknown | propel |
| training | Eagle | Uranus | freezing | navigate |
| triathlon | commander | Neptune | profound | communicate |
| spacewalk | splashdown | meteor | historic | train |
| father | humble | Moon | breathtaking | eclipse |

# VOCABULARY VAULT

## Stone Age

| Neanderthal | Mammoth | Nouns | Adjectives | Verbs |
|---|---|---|---|---|
| caveman | tusk | spear | beastly | shelter |
| primitive | hunted | weapon | thundering | destroy |
| bone | clothing | civilisation | unintelligent | hunt |
| hunter | weapons | survival | lethal | cook |
| gatherer | dangerous | glacier | primitive | survive |
| shelter | deadly | shelter | rugged | track |
| forest | enormous | evolution | natural | forage |
| artwork | extinct | nomad | fertile | gather |
| tribe | forager | Neanderthal | filthy | skin |
| Skara Brae | mammal | artefact | tenacious | evolve |

## Suffragettes

| Suffragette | E. Pankhurst | Noun | Adjectives | Verbs |
|---|---|---|---|---|
| movement | leader | Emily Davison | violent | vote |
| protest | political | women | radical | strike |
| politics | activist | union | persistent | handcuff |
| suffrage | strong | sympathy | selfless | transcend |
| vote | imprisoned | martyr | determined | suffer |
| campaign | persuade | election | willing | trigger |
| equal | contributor | rights | unwavering | spur |
| opportunities | legacy | suffrage | intense | perpetuate |
| fighting | significant | labour | militant | battle |
| tactical | selfless | King's horse | resolute | endure |

# VOCABULARY VAULT

## Superheroes

| Spiderman | Batman | Superman | Wonder Woman | Mindset |
|-----------|--------|----------|--------------|---------|
| Peter Parker | Bruce Wayne | Clark Kent | Diana Prince | intelligent |
| climb | utility belt | Lois Lane | Amazonian | brave |
| web | batmobile | Daily Planet | Themyscira | tactical |
| bite | lair | kryptonite | shield | determined |
| venom | sidekick | Krypton | Lasso of Truth | selfless |
| agility | Robin | cape | sword | energetic |
| senses | Alfred | fly | Ares | fearless |
| spider | Gotham City | Lex Luther | armour | isolated |
| arachnid | villains | reporter | bracelets | generous |
| teenager | orphan | glasses | boomerang | courageous |

## The Maya

| Conquistador | Warrior | Noun | Adjectives | Verbs |
|--------------|---------|------|------------|-------|
| Spanish | well-trained | Armada | ambitious | invent |
| metallic | loyal | art | primitive | fight |
| armoured | fearless | Maya | outstanding | observe |
| powerful | indigenous | trade | exceptional | destroy |
| smallpox | tribes | maize | deadly | infect |
| firearms | lifetime | medicine | educated | observe |
| artillery | training | Chichen-Itza | greedy | trick |
| animals | headdress | warrior | ruthless | defend |
| tactics | savage | ceramics | naive | sacrifice |
| warfare | animal pelt | astronomy | sophisticated | abandon |

Vocabulary Ninja © Andrew Jennings, 2024

# VOCABULARY VAULT

## Titanic

| Edward Smith | Sinking | Nouns | Adjectives | Verbs |
|---|---|---|---|---|
| Captain | Southampton | death | infamous | save |
| perished | New York | collision | glorious | collide |
| White Star Line | iceberg | merchant | luxurious | float |
| SS Celtic | North Atlantic | passenger | foundering | survive |
| Baltic | 2,224 on board | life vest | horror | inflate |
| Adriatic | lifeboats | iceberg | broad | obliterate |
| Olympic | collision | wreck | unsinkable | gouge |
| adversity | starboard | disaster | spacious | breach |
| hero | 1,500 died | tragedy | doomed | freeze |
| immersed | ill-prepared | superliner | regal | die |

## Toys

| Victorian | Modern | Noun | Adjectives | Verbs |
|---|---|---|---|---|
| yo-yo | tablet | blow football | new | play |
| pop gun | Lego | Atari | fun | flick |
| whip and top | Hatchimals | train set | old | move |
| cup and ball | Nintendo | Twister | colourful | touch |
| Jacob's ladder | Xbox | tiddlywinks | interesting | bounce |
| marbles | trading cards | Etch-a-Sketch | handmade | remember |
| wooden blocks | scooter | He-Man | musical | love |
| hopscotch | Paw Patrol Toys | Care Bear | stuffed | laugh |
| doll's house | fidget spinner | pogo stick | beautiful | argue |
| rocking horse | Transformers | Barbie | expensive | score |

# VOCABULARY VAULT

## Tudors

| Henry VIII | Wives | Nouns | Adjectives | Verbs |
|---|---|---|---|---|
| strong | Catherine of Aragon | gallows | ruthless | marry |
| athletic | Anne Boleyn | hood | insolent | joust |
| sportsman | Jane Seymour | lute | promiscuous | behead |
| tennis | Anne of Cleves | executioner | elegant | execute |
| jousting | Katherine Howard | peasant | lustful | break-up |
| educated | Katherine Parr | trial | talented | abolish |
| Latin | divorced | gargoyle | attractive | annul |
| obesity | beheaded | chemise | playful | divorce |
| charismatic | executed | banquet | jealous | tax |
| insecure | survived | scythe | turbulent | murder |

## Victorians

| Queen Victoria | Charles Darwin | Noun | Adjectives | Verbs |
|---|---|---|---|---|
| monarch | scientist | dunce cap | oppressive | explore |
| 1837 – 1901 | theory | mangle | dirty | diagnose |
| cousin married | evolution | steam engine | literary | maintain |
| 9 children | HMS Beagle | marbles | impressive | overcrowd |
| author | specimen | science | enlightened | design |
| artist | voyage | washboard | polluted | pioneer |
| languages | animal | chalk | eloquent | teach |
| penny black | plant | cane | loving | dwell |
| Victoria Cross | study | factory | sporty | employ |
| jubilee | botany | camera | prosperous | manufacture |

# VOCABULARY VAULT

## Vikings

| Rollo | Erik the Red | Warrior | Adjectives | Verbs |
|---|---|---|---|---|
| leader | red hair | fierce | murderous | intimidate |
| raids | hot temper | honour | horrific | invade |
| France | banished | raider | enraged | exploit |
| 9th century | manslaughter | monks | ruthless | unleash |
| Normandy | explorer | Valhalla | intelligent | navigate |
| invasion | settler | cultured | unkempt | settle |
| protector | colonist | burial | intrepid | capture |
| descendants | untamed | long ship | destructive | voyage |
| voyage | founder | Karl and Jarl | tactical | conquer |
| giant | killer | myths | rough | stalk |

## Volcanoes

| Mt. St. Helens | Mt. Vesuvius | Mt. Etna | Adjectives | Verbs |
|---|---|---|---|---|
| 2,549 metres | 1,281 metres | 3,320 metres | intense | eject |
| Washington State | famous | Sicily | volcanic | scorch |
| USA | infamous | Italy | infernal | plume |
| monument | active | active | dangerous | choke |
| Skamania | Italy | rich soil | ferocious | spiral |
| County | Naples | tourism | mesmeric | smother |
| active | Pompeii | Mongibello | formidable | overwhelm |
| avalanche | 79 AD | popular | colossal | explode |
| destruction | Herculaneum | sleeping | cataclysmic | burn |
| disaster | stratovolcano | monster | unstoppable | shatter |

# VOCABULARY VAULT

## Water cycle

| Water cycle | Processes | Nouns | Adjectives | Verbs |
|---|---|---|---|---|
| water | evaporation | mountain | peaceful | monitor |
| rain | transpiration | stream | frozen | trap |
| roots | precipitation | gas | muddy | cycle |
| sun | condensation | flood | natural | return |
| wind | filter | weather | relaxing | condense |
| snow | run-off | wildlife | wondrous | precipitate |
| lake | collection | tributaries | mighty | meander |
| river | transport | lake | narrow | pour |
| sea | storage | cycle | broad | flow |
| water vapour | atmosphere | ocean | dry | rise |

## World War I

| Lloyd George | Wilhelm II | Noun | Adjectives | Verbs |
|---|---|---|---|---|
| Prime Minister | Emperor | RAF | inhuman | murder |
| solicitor | King | USSR | nightmarish | negotiate |
| opposed | abdicated | Great War | nauseating | persecute |
| conscription | ineffective | Germany | emotional | revenge |
| mediate | fled | Austria | cowardly | execute |
| frustrated | republic | U-boat | fatal | survive |
| Allies | exile | Bully Beef | murderous | bomb |
| strategic | Prussia | France | loathsome | defend |
| appeasement | shocked | RMS Lusitania | bloody | invade |
| charming | Third Reich | battlefield | heroic | lead |

# PART 3
## BE THE VOCABULARY NINJA

# CONCLUSION

Words can be awe-inspiring, devastatingly painful, comfortingly unforgettable, intoxicating, humbling and so much more. Words are everything to me; words can be indescribably powerful for you. This is the esteem in which you now need to hold words – one where you hold them up to the highest level of importance in your classroom. Everyone has the potential to become a Vocabulary Ninja in body and mind. And, although this might feel like the end of our journey together, it's actually only the very beginning!

As this part of our journey together ends, you must start the next exciting instalment of becoming a Vocabulary Ninja by yourself. But you will never really be alone: I will always be here to support you, guide you and celebrate with you – just look on social media and you will always find me.

Recently, I was forced to look a little deeper into the definition of what a ninja actually is, and what the word itself means (yes, I hear the irony screaming loud and clear). Quite simply:

## *'A ninja is a person who excels in a particular skill or activity.'*

No matter the context – whether it be dancing, singing, drawing, cooking, playing sport or bringing words to life as a Vocabulary Ninja – no one can realistically expect to excel in a particular skill or activity without having the right mindset and the dedication to make their goals a reality. When you look at a skilled musician or sports person, you look on in awe as they execute their skills to perfection; they make it look easy. What you don't see is the meticulous preparation, the energy-sapping training or practice sessions, the heartbreaking disappointments and frustrations along the way. This will be true of your journey to become a Vocabulary Ninja teacher. Remember your training. Be micro-ambitious and strive for those marginal gains in every learning opportunity; the sum of all the small parts is where you will find your victory and have the greatest impact.

Who knows where the journey will take you? You are the trailblazing Grasshopper who is about to become a Vocabulary Ninja for yourself, your pupils and your school, and for that I applaud you. Believe it or not, your new focus will have an impact quickly: it will be noticed by the staff and pupils in your school. The word will spread! At this point, you will no longer be a Grasshopper, you will be Shinobi, and staff members will come to you for guidance to ask how you did it. It is then your responsibility to spread the Vocabulary Ninja mindset to *your* Grasshoppers. Truly, words will now have the power to unlock the doors to a whole new world of understanding in your school!

Good luck, although, I foresee that you will not need it.

# ADDITIONAL RESOURCES

Digital resources are essential in any modern classroom. Here are some fabulous resources that could help pupils make independent vocabulary choices when they might be struggling.

## WEBSITES

There are some brilliant resources around the web that can help you in your quest to improve pupils' vocabulary. Here are some of Vocabulary Ninja's favourites to get you started.

### 1 – Describing Words

**www.describingwords.io**
A wonderful resource for staff and pupils to access. The tool simply generates describing words (adjectives) for you to use.

### 2 – LiteracyShed / Spelling Shed

**www.literacyshed.com**
A vault of fantastic videos, perfect for inspiring writing. All with teaching ideas and techniques!

### 3 – Pobble365 and Pobble

**www.pobble.com**
Pobble is a terrific resource for supercharging pupils' writing and creating a genuine audience for it. Pobble 365 offers a picture each and every day of the year with associated teaching ideas.

### 4 – Collins Online Dictionary

**www.collinsdictionary.com**
A fabulously comprehensive dictionary resource with detailed yet child-friendly definitions of words, complete with examples, pronunciations and much more.

### 5 – NiftyWord

**www.niftyword.com**
Simply type in a word and NiftyWord will present you with associated suffixes, prefixes and related words! Super simple, but super effective.

### 6 – Online Etymology Dictionary

**www.etymonline.com**
Explore the etymology of any word you can imagine.

### 7 – Word Hippo

**www.wordhippo.com**
Explore synonyms, antonyms, meanings, rhyming and much more.

### 8 – Snappy Words

**www.snappywords.com**
An online visual dictionary and thesaurus.

### 9 – Lexipedia

**www.lexipedia.com**
A visual online synonym programme that displays associated words.

### 10 – Chat GTP

**www.chat.openai.com**
Ask Chat GTP to explain words and write model sentences and texts for pupils to read. Make sure to check its work before sharing with your class!

## REFERENCES

Beck, I. L., McKeown, M. G., Kucan, L. (2013). Bringing Words to Life: Robust Vocabulary Instruction. United Kingdom: Guilford Publications.

Hart, B. and Risley, T. R. (2003) 'The early catastrophe', *Education Review*, 17(1), pp 110–118.

# ANSWERS

## NOUN VS VERB

**Decide if the target word is being used as a noun or a verb.**

| Target word | Context | Word class |
|---|---|---|
| crush | There was a crush in the corridor before playtime. | noun |
| bottle | We needed to bottle as much water as possible. | verb |
| paint | Everyone used the paint with care and attention. | noun |
| watch | His watch had stopped working. | noun |
| block | He raised his hand to block the sunlight. | verb |
| arm | They need to arm themselves before the battle begins. | verb |
| picture | He couldn't picture everybody playing nicely together. | verb |
| level | Jimmy used the spade to level off the ground. | verb |
| clap | Mr Rogers could hear a clap, but wasn't sure where. | noun |
| peel | Next to the bin, there was lots of fruit peel on the floor. | noun |
| spoon | Helen was asked to spoon the sand into the tray. | verb |
| fire | There was a huge fire which could be seen for miles. | noun |
| light | As it was bedtime, Alex needed to switch off his light. | noun |
| dip | Peter wanted to dip his biscuit into the warm tea. | verb |
| cover | The book cover was tatty and frayed at the edges. | noun |
| book | Mum needed to book the tickets before they left. | verb |
| train | We need to train harder if we are to win the competition. | verb |
| frown | My frown just couldn't be turned upside down. | noun |

# SPaG FACTS

| Give examples of these types of word. | | | |
|---|---|---|---|
| noun | any person, place, thing | possessive pronoun | my, our, his, her, your |
| verb | any being, doing, having word | subordinating conjunction | until, while, since, etc. |
| adjective | any describing word | coordinating conjunction | for, and, nor, but, or, so |
| adverb | can be added to a verb | proper noun | person, place or thing with capital letter |
| pronoun | his, her, he, she, I, me, us | collective noun | clan, herd, pack, troop |
| article | a, an, the | abstract noun | truth, danger, happiness |
| determiner | a, an, the, this, that, these | concrete noun | bell, sky, blanket |
| preposition | in, on, under, inside, next to | quantifier | some, any, many, few |

| Rewrite these words in their expanded form. | |
|---|---|
| can't | cannot |
| isn't | is not |
| won't | will not |
| couldn't | could not |
| mustn't | must not |
| didn't | did not |
| I'll | I will |

| Rewrite these words in the past tense. | |
|---|---|
| kick | kicked |
| move | moved |
| catch | caught |
| remain | remained |
| fight | fought |
| perform | performed |
| blow | blew |

| Circle apostrophes for possession. | |
|---|---|
| Jenny's car | We mustn't |
| I'll be late | Mark's dinner |
| The man's hat | Don't |

| Circle the modal verbs. | |
|---|---|
| would | might |
| fill | park |
| should | may |

# ANSWERS

## SPaG FACTS

| Give examples of these types of word. | | | |
|---|---|---|---|
| noun | any person, place, thing | possessive pronoun | my, our, his, her, your |
| verb | any being, doing, having word | subordinating conjunction | until, while, since, etc. |
| adjective | any describing word | coordinating conjunction | for, and, nor, but, or, so |
| adverb | can be added to a verb | proper noun | person, place or thing with capital letter |
| pronoun | his, her, he, she, I, me, us | collective noun | clan, herd, pack, troop |
| article | a, an, the | abstract noun | truth, danger, happiness |
| determiner | a, an, the, this, that, these | concrete noun | bell, sky, blanket |
| preposition | in, on, under, inside, next to | quantifier | some, any, many, few |

| Add punctuation accurately. | |
|---|---|
| , | Under the table, the slimy frog jumped onto my foot. |
| . | I love ice cream. |
| ? | Who is it? |
| ! | What a day! |
| ( ) | Mr Dot (the teacher) was eating his lunch. |
| " " | "Get lost," boomed the man. |
| ; | We couldn't be beaten; it just couldn't happen. |

| Add an appropriate prefix. | |
|---|---|
| dis | believe |
| anti | freeze |
| aero | plane |
| pre | paid |
| dis | charge |
| re | fill |
| un | usual |

| Add the capital letters, commas and full stops. |
|---|
| Yesterday, we went for lunch with Mr Johnson, Jenny and Phillip. |

| Circle subordinating conjunctions. | |
|---|---|
| (until) | (whether) |
| regret | fool |
| (although) | (since) |

# SPaG SPOTTER

**Circle the relevant part of speech.**

| Can you spot…? | Context |
|---|---|
| the nouns | The boys were playing football in the park with their friends. |
| the verbs | Clean up your room and help your sister with her homework. |
| the adjectives | The crumbling mountain couldn't support the delicate ecosystem. |
| the adverbs | Singing loudly, I was completely relaxed. |
| the articles | I would love to have a friend like you. |
| the determiner | If only I could find those comfortable slippers. |
| the prepositions | Jamal was perched on the table while Alex hid under the table. |
| a coordinating conjunction | We were all ready to leave, but Fred had forgotten his bag. |
| the pronouns | She was so cool; I admired her so much. |
| a subordinating conjunction | Although it was late, Paul wanted to stay up to watch the film. |
| a noun phrase | I could see lots of yummy, cold yoghurt. |

**Edit the sentence to make it correct.**

| Can you add…? | Context |
|---|---|
| a comma to make a fronted adverbial | Even though she was tall, I knew I could still beat her. |
| commas in the list | Even Derek, Gina, Kazuki and Mark were going to the party. |
| a / an | The class dearly wanted to adopt an elephant. |
| brackets | Mr Hill (the class teacher) was determined to beat the children. |
| the capital letters | Underneath the Manchester skyline, Jenny could see Mary crying. |